AGE NICOLAISEN

THE POCKET ENCYCLOPAEDIA OF INDOOR PLANTS IN COLOUR

Illustrated by
PALLE BREGNHOI and OTTO FRELLO

Edited by
RICHARD GORER

BLANDFORD   PRESS
Poole   Dorset

First published in the U.K. 1970
by Blandford Press, Link House,
West Street, Poole, Dorset BH15 1LL

English text Copyright © 1970 Blandford Books Ltd.
Reprinted 1971
Reprinted 1973
Reprinted 1981

ISBN 0 7137 01145

World Copyright © 1969
Politikens Forlag A/S
Copenhagen, Denmark

Printed in Hong Kong by South China Printing Co.

PREFACE

This replaces the highly successful INDOOR PLANTS IN COLOUR in this series which has already appeared in three impressions. The text is by a different author and the new illustrations have been drawn specially for this edition.

As with some of the other books in this same series, this volume first appeared in Scandinavia. As more and more English books are read outside the British Isles, and as this subject in particular is one of great popularity in Australasia and on the American Continent, where these books will be read, it is therefore appropriate that the range of plants illustrated and described and the conditions for their culture have a rather broader concept than a purely British one.

Indeed, the condition inside houses is constantly changing with the increasing use of central heating, and therefore many of the temperatures given originally for a Scandinavian environment are increasingly relevant for more temperate climates. In view of the worldwide readership no attempt has been made to edit the book for a particular country, but the reader is invited to bear this in mind when studying the text.

Both greenhouse owners and growers of house-plants will find this book of great interest. Occasionally the treatment suggested may differ a little from that followed in some other countries, and it will be interesting to see if readers obtain better results in following the Danish author's suggestions.

It will be noted, for instance, that the author suggests a much more extensive use of soilless mixtures (i.e. loamless composts) than is sometimes practised. Moreover, when they are used, there is usually little additional feeding for the first year.

Mr. Nicolaisen seems to employ liquid feeds immediately and, presumably, in this way the fertility of the soilless mixture is maintained. With good loam becoming ever scarcer it is understandable that the standard potting composts, such as John Innes, are becoming increasingly difficult to produce in quantity and expensive to purchase. However, on the few occasions when our author does postulate a loam-based compost, one will be quite justified in using the John Innes Potting compost. It is usual also to use this compost for several woody plants such as the various Ficus and Palms, for which soilless mixture is suggested here. If plants are purchased that are growing in a loam-based compost, it is advisable to pot them on in a similar mixture. Composts that contain loam do not combine well with soilless mixtures and vice versa.

Most growers tend to use proprietary liquid fertilisers and these have the appropriate dosage marked on their containers. However, if you feel inclined to use your own liquid fertiliser mixture (see p. 145), you will certainly save money.

It will be noted that the majority of suggested feeds are for $\frac{1}{4}$ oz., $\frac{1}{2}$ oz., $\frac{3}{4}$ oz., and 1 oz. of the mixed chemicals per gallon of water. It is simplest to make a gallon with 1 oz. of the chemicals and dilute it to make the weaker mixtures. Thus, if you consider that you will want a pint at $\frac{1}{2}$ oz. per gallon, pour out half a pint of the mixture and add half a pint of water. In a few instances quantities larger than 1 oz. per gallon are suggested. In these cases you can either make a gallon of the stronger fertiliser or add a small quantity of the chemicals to your 1 oz. per gallon mixture. The reference to liquid feed throughout the text is to this mixture. Specific quantities are given for each plant.

Many of the temperatures recommended are somewhat on the high side for most homes and it has been found that many of the plants will survive happily at somewhat lower temperatures than those recommended here. Ficus and Philodendrons are quite happy at a winter temperature of 10–13°C. (50–55°F.) and in most cases it will be safe to grow the plants somewhat cooler than suggested here. On the other hand, no possible harm will accrue by following the suggested temperatures. The only query we have is the very low resting temperature suggested for *Clerodendron thomsoniae*. This may well prove very satisfactory, but in most greenhouses the temperature is not allowed to fall much below 10°C. (50°F.) for this plant.

One or two of the flowering times appear slightly unusual. In Britain *Viburnum tinus* will flower outside from November to April and is usually well over by May, which is given as the flowering time here. However, most of these doubtful statements have been left as the author wrote them. One or two obvious errors have been corrected, but where there was any room for doubt the author's text has been left unamended.

English vernacular names are given where they are in common and frequent use, but I have refrained from made-up names where they are not generally used.

RICHARD GORER

FOREWORD

This book, which is intended first and foremost as a work of reference for 'indoor gardeners', i.e. amateurs who cultivate plants indoors, in window boxes, or conservatories, lists and describes 350 different indoor plants. One hundred and fifty of the plants dealt with are illustrated by colour plates, while a further 100 are shown in black—white—green illustrations along with the plant descriptions. One hundred plants are not illustrated, since they so closely resemble the others that this is not considered necessary.

The plants shown in the colour plates are numbered from 1 to 150, and the number of each is given in the plant description immediately after its name for easy cross-reference.

In arranging the plants in sequence, the botanical system has been followed closely, both in the colour plates and in the plant descriptions. Within each family, the different species have, as far as is reasonably possible, been listed alphabetically. But in a few instances, it was more appropriate to give a description of the most popular subject, the growth and culture of which is of such importance that it has been printed outside the alphabetical sequence.

The book is prefaced by a short introduction concerning indoor plants, their use and care, along with some indications of the culture requirements of the plants. This is followed by the colour plates and the plant descriptions, set out on an identical basic pattern which includes the name of the family and species, habitat, growth, use, culture requirements and other details of care, pests and diseases, so that the reader may easily find the information he requires, whether he wishes to identify an unknown plant or obtain information on use and care. The book's function as a work of reference is augmented by a comprehensive index.

With regard to the indication of names, the family name is given in its official Latin form, while the names of the genus and species are both given in Latin and English wherever possible. In the English edition, the R.H.S. *Dictionary of Gardening* has been consulted.

The plants were selected and the text prepared by Cand. Hort. Åge Nicolaisen, a municipal gardener, while the illustrations are the work of artists Palle Bregnhøi and Otto Frello. Both the illustrations and the names of the plants have been checked by botanical gardeners at the Copenhagen University botanical gardens, Cand. Hort. Ernst Floto and Dendrology Professor at the Royal College of Agriculture and Veterinary

Science in Copenhagen, Dr. Phil. Johan Lange, to whom the editor is most indebted.

The book may be used internationally, and will be published in Britain, France, Holland, Italy, Norway, Spain, Sweden, Germany and the United States.

INTRODUCTION

THE TERM 'INDOOR PLANTS'

The term covers all foliage and flowering plants which can be cultivated indoors on window-sills, in special flower windows or bay windows, in halls, on staircases, on verandas, or in patios and conservatories.

All types of plants can be used as indoor plants: trees and bushes, shrubs, bulbous and tuberous plants and annuals. This great variety means that use and care are subject to all kinds of different requirements. Some indoor plants can be kept indoors for many years in the same situation; other types are seasonal and must be discarded after flowering. The same plant may behave differently in different climatic conditions. One plant may, for example, be tree-like in tropical regions, where there is no great fluctuation in climate, whereas it may be cultivated or may thrive as a sub-shrub in temperate regions—in colder climates even as an annual.

This irregularity may also be encountered where the plant is cultivated indoors in an artificial climate. The intensity of the light and relative degree of air humidity, in particular, may vary here so greatly that certain plants appear under some conditions to be tree-like perennials, while under different conditions they may be short-lived herbaceous plants. The reason why certain indoor plants often fare badly is not therefore necessarily lack of skill on the part of the gardener but rather the wrong climate in the room or winter garden.

CHOICE OF INDOOR PLANTS

An 'indoor gardener' naturally wants his plants to grow as well as possible, and beginners must therefore start with the 'easy' varieties. The more experienced, on the other hand, may like to try their skill with plants whose culture and care impose particularly exacting demands, and the choice of plants in this book takes both groups into account. The plant descriptions make it clear whether the plant is an 'easy' or 'difficult' one, and warnings are given against trying out certain varieties which do not normally thrive under indoor cultivation. Enthusiasts are encouraged to try out new plants and to specialise in types which present a particular challenge to their skills. There are indoor gardeners who have concentrated on orchids, and others who have specialised in ferns, plants of the pineapple family (bromeliads) or cacti. There are infinite possibilities which this book may perhaps stimulate the reader to try.

Thousands of plants can be cultivated in an artificial indoor climate, but the selection presented here only covers those which are generally cultivated or may reasonably be expected to be obtainable from nurserymen. Many of the plants dealt with are not grown in the large nurseries, but must be looked for among the small commercial gardeners who grow a large and varied range. It may be that some can only be bought as seeds from home or foreign seed merchants, or may have to be obtained from botanical gardens.

In the plant descriptions the country or place of origin is given, often with a short description of the local geographic or climatic conditions, which may provide the reader with a picture of the cultural requirements or possibilities for use indoors. The appearance of the plants is only briefly indicated, and the text must therefore be read in conjunction with the colour plates or the illustrations appearing with the plant descriptions. The most important characteristics, however, as for example growth form, leaves, flowers, fragrance if any, fruit and height of indoor culture, are included.

An indication is also given as to whether the plant is particularly suitable for cultivation in an ordinary window-box, in a conservatory or under extreme conditions, such as deep shade or burning sun. Possibilities for growth out of doors during the summer as a balcony or tub plant are also mentioned. Information is given as to whether the plant is a perennial indoor variety or a seasonal type which must be discarded after flowering.

Within each species there are often quite a few different varieties which may make for a pleasant change in the window-box. In such cases the most important varieties are mentioned, with an indication of varying flower or leaf colours or other special characteristics.

The Englerian system has been followed closely in the order in which the plants have been arranged, both in the colour plates and in the plant descriptions. Botanical research, however, is constantly bringing about changes in the sequence applied in the system, and a book such as this can therefore only remain in conformity with the correct official system for a short time. Since, for technical reasons, the illustrations and descriptions cannot be relocated in each new edition, we have decided to follow a single, slightly older system, specially adapted to the indoor gardener's requirements, but which does not incorporate the most recent decisions of the International Botanical Congress.

THE CULTURE REQUIREMENTS OF INDOOR PLANTS

Indoor plants impose a wide variety of demands on soil, fertiliser, water, light, heat and air, which are all detailed under the appropriate headings in the individual plant descriptions.

In an ordinary room it will usually only be possible to satisfy these demands approximately. Homes are primarily intended to meet the needs and wishes of those who live in them rather than the requirements of plants which may be kept there, so it is not surprising that an indoor atmosphere often does not suit the plant at all well. The size of the window may limit the intensity of the light, and central heating makes for high temperatures and air which is too dry, an atmosphere in which some plants fare particularly badly.

The combination of climatic factors is possibly even more important than the individual factors alone. It may thus be of little use to have the right temperature if there is not the corresponding optimum amount of light and air humidity in the room. Cacti, for example, thrive outstandingly well in dry, centrally heated air, but the amount of light in rooms is much too small during most months of the year.

By changing the temperature and air humidity, by ensuring the right degree of soil moisture, by adding artificial light and by applying the correct dosage of nutrition to the pot soil, one can get very close to the optimum conditions for some indoor plants, but these conditions may not suit the other plants which are being cultivated in the room. The room atmosphere must therefore remain a compromise which takes account first and foremost of the people who live there, and then of the plants.

Soil

The pot soil must be thoroughly porous, so that air and moisture can easily penetrate. An artificially blended soilless mixture can be bought which consists of peat with the most important nutrient materials added. This suits many plant types, but where experience has shown that plants fare badly in such a mixture, this is expressly indicated in the descriptions. Otherwise, the enthusiast may make an excellent potting soil for himself by mixing a good, light loam with peat, well-rotted manure and fine grit or sharp sand.

Plants which make special demands on the composition of the soil are most often those with a poorly developed root system, or with roots which thrive best under particular chemical conditions, for example acid soil with a low reaction rate (denoted by pH), or in an especially alkaline soil with a high reaction rate. Neutral soil has a rate of pH 7, acid soil down to pH 3 and alkaline soil up to pH 8.

The reaction rate of a soil blend can be raised by the addition of calcium or simply by watering with ordinary tap water, which usually has a high calcium content, and can be lowered by the addition of 'acid' nutrients, such as potassium sulphate. Most indoor plants like a soil mixture with a reaction rate which is not too alkaline; therefore, on daily watering, 1 gram of ammonium sulphate per litre ($\frac{1}{4}$ oz. per gallon) should be added to keep the reaction rate suitably low.

Mixing in sand makes the soil lighter, but at the same time it will then dry out more quickly, so it must be watered frequently. The addition of peat brings about an increased capacity for the absorption of moisture, so a soil of this type does not need such frequent watering. The porosity of the soil can be increased, without altering its chemical composition, by adding such materials as 'Styromuld', 'Perlite' or 'Vermiculite'.

If ordinary clay flower-pots are used, a considerable amount of evaporation from the surface of the pot must be expected, whereas plastic pots allow only a small amount of evaporation or none at all. Plants requiring constant moisture at their roots thus do especially well in plastic pots.

Feeding

The soil content of a flower-pot is very small and, depending on the appetite of the plant in question, the nutrient materials it contains are used up after a certain period of time. Therefore care should be taken to feed the plants at the appropriate intervals. Some plants should be given small quantities of nourishment at short but regular intervals; other, more demanding varieties must be given larger amounts at longer intervals. One or two plants hardly need to be fed at all, but prefer their soil to be changed completely every year or six months. Nourishment in powder form should *never* be given with dry pot soil, so make sure that the soil is thoroughly moist beforehand, otherwise there is a danger that the artificial fertiliser may scorch the roots. It is easier to apply a liquid fertiliser, which is added to the water and can be used on dry soil.

Any one of the mixed fertilisers available from dealers may be used for nourishment. These have closely controlled contents of the three main nutrient materials, nitrogen, potassium and phosphorus, and also contain small amounts of the necessary trace elements such as manganese, magnesium, iron, boron and many others.

It is just as easy—and considerably cheaper—to make your own fertiliser mixture. This may consist of 100 grams (3 oz.) of potassium nitrate, 100 grams (3 oz.) of calcium phosphate and 200 grams (6 oz.) of ammonium sulphate. All three chemicals can be purchased from a chemist and mixed together, but they must be kept dry, otherwise the mixture becomes lumpy. The powder dissolves easily in water, and with each application 1–3 grams per litre ($\frac{1}{4}$–1 oz. per gallon) should be used, as specified in the individual plant descriptions.

Do not use too much fertiliser, as this will scorch the roots. On the other hand, if too little is used, there is the danger that the plant will be stunted in its growth. Never feed young seedlings, newly re-potted plants or diseased plants, and never administer nourishment during the darkest period of the winter, when the plant is not able to use and convert the salts in the fertiliser.

Some plants need special treatment with acid nutrition, and this is indicated in the descriptions dealing with these particular types.

In order to give particularly vigorous plants a good start, what is known as a *basic nutrient* may be given, which consists of mixing a long-acting fertiliser in with the pot soil itself before planting. For this, you can use any good, natural organic fertiliser.

Water

A large percentage of every plant consists of water, which is a vital requirement since plants absorb all forms of nourishment dissolved in water, and can only breathe and assimilate in a certain level of air humidity.

In nature, water penetrates through the surface of the soil and down to the plant's roots where it is absorbed. The best method of watering is therefore in most cases to administer the water from above on to the soil ball. Some plants will not tolerate water in the soil, and it is best to water them through base dishes. Any water which the plant has not been able to absorb in the space of half an hour must be poured away. Many species of the pineapple family have very weakly developed roots, and it is best to water them through the central growth.

Tap water often contains calcium or disinfectants, such as chlorine, which plants as a rule do not like. Calcium in the water changes the acid level in the soil, and ugly spots may be produced on leaves and stems; rainwater—or some other calcium-free water—should therefore be used, and indeed this is essential in the case of some plants such as azaleas, camellias or gardenias.

Water must always have the chill taken off it, since the use of ice-cold tap water can give plants a 'cold shock'. Most plants should always be given water at room temperature, up to minimum $16°$ C. ($65°$ F.).

Many plants have a rhythmic life cycle, alternating between periods of growth and rest. Resting periods tend to coincide either with the winter or with the dry season of the plant's native habitat, and if the resting period corresponds to our own winter the plants may be less suitable for us, since we prefer indoor plants which flower and grow green at that time. This only applies to herbaceous or deciduous plants. However, the selection of plants in this book covers a range of varieties with a life cycle of this kind, which are such splendid plants indoors and in conservatories, as well as on terraces and in window-boxes, that we would not wish to leave them out and, for practical reasons, must include them in the indoor plants category.

The following might be a basic rule for watering: Give plenty of water each time, and let the pot soil dry out almost completely between each watering. Watering in dribbles is as bad as no watering at all.

Light

All green plants require light in order to be able to grow and develop. Sunlight may be replaced by artificial light, but for ordinary conditions this need not be taken into consideration.

A plant's need for a large amount of light does not always coincide with its capacity to tolerate direct sunlight. Diffused light, i.e. without direct sunshine, provides even and agreeable lighting for many plants. A large window facing north, provided there are no buildings casting a shadow or shrubbery outside, is an excellent growth spot for many plants. But, generally speaking, north-facing windows tend to look out on to neighbouring houses or dense shrubbery, and for that reason only plants which are amenable to shade are likely to thrive in these locations.

Windows facing east or west usually offer the best possibilities for the cultivation of indoor plants. In windows facing south, only plants which require both a high light intensity and high daytime temperatures are likely to do well. It is often an advantage to shade the flower-pot against direct sunlight, so that the pot soil does not heat up too much thereby scorching the plant's roots.

Where plants have a pronounced dependence on the length of the day, it is possible to vary this artificially by creating darkness during light periods and providing additional light during dark periods, thus influencing the flowering pattern. Some in this category we call short-day plants—those which flower when the day is less than twelve hours long—and others long-day plants—those which produce buds when night is shorter than day.

Heat

The vast majority of indoor plants need a temperature of over $0°$ C. ($32°$ F.) and die when exposed to frost. Some, especially tropical varieties, are so sensitive that they suffer slight damage at temperatures below minimum $10°$ C. ($50°$ F.). On the other hand, they can withstand quite high temperatures, as long as the level of air humidity and the right amount of water enables them to do so.

During the resting periods most plants require lower temperatures than during their growth period. Even 'all-year-round' plants have a certain rhythm, and prefer lower temperatures during the dark season. This may be difficult to provide for in living-rooms with central heating; we, after all, prefer higher room temperatures during the winter. The ideal indoor plants are therefore those which thrive best in living areas with unnatural climatic conditions during the winter.

No indoor plant thrives next to a stove or above a coal fire, and only very few grow well above a radiator.

Air

The reason for the recent fashion for house plants is to be sought in our changed patterns of living. In former times in old houses the doors and windows were so poorly sealed that damp air from outside penetrated in against the heated room air, and if there is a growth factor of special importance to plants it is the degree of humidity in the air.

The air in centrally heated rooms is very dry, and must be made more humid by sprinkling the plant with lukewarm water, using either an aerosol or a syringe. Weekly sponging of the leaves removes dust and gives them a better chance of functioning; during the summer this is best achieved by leaving the plants to stand outside on a rainy day.

Very few plants will tolerate draughts, and should therefore not be placed near doors and windows which are often opened.

OTHER FORMS OF CARE REQUIRED

Besides trying to satisfy the various culture requirements of indoor plants as best one can, daily care also involves a number of indoor gardeners' chores which are of additional importance to their well-being. These include re-potting, pruning, supporting, propagation and protection against pests and diseases.

Daily care

While attending daily to the plants—giving water and any nourishment required and providing supports where necessary—it is also important to remove withered leaves, flowers and shoots if these are seen.

At intervals one should also break up the surface soil in the pot, so that it remains porous and easy for water to penetrate. Many indoor plants, however, have roots which are so close to the surface that they would be destroyed by this procedure. Instead it is possible to 'top-dress' these varieties, i.e. cover the pot soil with a very thin layer of loamless compost, peat or something similar.

Re-potting

Vigorous indoor plants use up the nutrients in the soil relatively fast. Even where this nourishment is supplemented by added fertiliser, the roots must from time to time have fresh soil. On the one hand, chemicals may become precipitated in the soil, so that the roots are scorched, and on the other hand, the physical structure of the soil changes, so that the roots have difficulty in forcing their way through and water and air cannot easily penetrate.

It is best to re-pot simultaneously with the start of the new growth in the early spring. Old, thickened roots should be removed carefully, and new basic fertiliser mixed into the fresh pot soil. At the same time, arrange for good drainage by laying crocks (i.e. broken pieces of flower-pot, crockery, etc.), sand or gravel in the bottom of the pot.

Water generously immediately after re-potting, but do not water too freely during the period which follows, until the new roots have developed. Avoid feeding altogether during the first two months after re-potting.

Pruning

Plants which have a tree-like growth must be pruned from time to time, partly so as to contain them in a restrained situation such as a confined window space and partly in order to promote better flowering or vegetative development. Pruning may be undertaken simultaneously with re-potting, but otherwise the best time is in the spring before new growth begins. Pruning may often provide material for propagation in the form of woody or herbaceous cuttings.

Stopping of herbaceous top shoots by means of pinching out the top-most shoots during the growth period promotes a better development of lateral branches, and in many cases also more luxuriant flowering.

Disbudding, which is for example used for chrysanthemums and roses involves the removal of side buds beneath a terminal bud so that the latter may grow particularly vigorously and give larger, better formed flowers.

Supports

Most indoor plants can do without supports. Large ornamental varieties such as Ficus, on the other hand, frequently need some kind of support, especially when they are kept in darker positions where the growth will automatically strive towards the light. The best support to use is a bamboo stick to which the plant is tied with raffia, string or 'Twist-it', thin steel wire wound with green paper.

Trellis plants, i.e. twining or climbing varieties, require some form of trellis upon which they can fasten. Some of them are equipped with tendrils or aerial roots; others cling by the stalks or leaf stems twining themselves around the trellis, which may consist of vertical and horizontal bamboo canes, trellis work made of steel wire, or a network made of fine-mesh fish netting.

Always take care that the string and trellis do not cut into parts of the plant.

PROPAGATION

A number of indoor plants can be propagated by simple division when re-potting, others by cuttings of side or top shoots, rooted into soil mixed with sand, for which a propagating unit is very suitable, with well sealed, humid air which will assist the developments of roots. By placing the plant-box or flower-pot containing the cuttings over 'bottom heat', for example above a radiator, more rapid root formation and development of the new plant is ensured. The use of root stimulating agents such as 'Seradix', 'Rootone' or 'Hormodin' greatly assists root formation in varieties which are otherwise difficult to propagate from cuttings in plant windows.

Finally, a number of indoor plants can be propagated by planting seeds; many of these can be bought from seed merchants and sown in flower-pots on window-sills in the spring.

PROTECTION AGAINST PESTS AND DISEASE

The most common pests are greenfly, mealy bugs, nematodes, scale insects, snails and slugs, red spider mites, springtails, thrips, wood lice and earwigs. These can be combated by spraying or dusting with 'Lindane' or the less toxic 'Malathion', which, however, must be used with care because of their poisonous effects. When giving this treatment, take the plants into a cellar, conservatory, or outdoors in mild weather; never treat them in the house itself. Minor attacks can be stopped before they have a drastic effect, but severely affected plants must be thrown out.

The most common diseases are grey mould, mildew, root rot and stem canker. These fungus diseases can be combated by spraying, dusting or watering with 'Thiram' or 'Captan': always follow carefully the instructions for use printed on the package.

The failure of indoor plants to grow satisfactorily, however, often stems from disrupting factors other than those caused by pests or fungus diseases. Damage from cold or frost, lack of light or damage from excess light, too much watering, use of water containing calcium, drought, scorching of roots resulting from incorrect feeding, top scorching and re-potting at the wrong time are the most common reasons why indoor plants fail to do well or take on a sickly appearance. Indoor gardeners must therefore concentrate in the first place on correct day-to-day care in order to obtain good results.

THE POSITION OF INDOOR PLANTS IN THE HOUSE

While the living-rooms in the newer houses often have built-in flower-troughs, there are few possibilities in an older house, with ordinary sills at each window, to grow a varied selection of indoor plants. These are kept in their pots in rows, the pots perhaps having special outer containers made of porcelain, ceramic material or copper. Plants must never be placed directly in these containers, however.

Special flower windows can be arranged by planting indoor plants in a watertight trough or container of soil, which is then placed on the window-sill, on the floor in front of the window or on a flower display table. Care must be taken to ensure that the container is sufficiently deep, since larger plants require at least 30 cm. (1 ft.) of soil. Flat boxes or dishes are unsuitable for planting, if the plants are to remain in them for extended periods without re-potting.

The ideal position for indoor plants is in a flower window, with glass between both the outside and the inside of the room. Between these two windows an artificial climate can be created with a suitably high temperature and degree of air humidity, which may suit many plants particularly well, especially the tropical and sub-tropical types. With the aid of a thermometer and humidity gauges, the atmosphere can be kept under control and regulated to the appropriate levels. In flower windows, the daylight can be supplemented during the dark season by artificial light from an electric light bulb or a fluorescent tube; this will promote growth and budding, and many plants will more easily overcome the inhibiting effects of winter darkness in this way. The climate in a flower window can be controlled using thermostats and other mechanical aids, and natural growth conditions reproduced for primeval forest plants, desert plants and others requiring special environments.

The flower window must be treated as a whole, so that the individual plants set each other off. It is an advantage not to select too many special types, but to keep to plants which belong to the same botanical or ecological group (plant community), because within these groups there are always varieties which also belong together aesthetically. Perhaps it is well to warn indoor gardeners against the procedure adopted by some flower decoration specialists in planting out so-called mixed flower arrangements. where special emphasis is placed on the contrast produced by the different leaf shapes and colours. flower shades or growth forms. A cheerful. green background for the general furnishing plan of the room is more important in the choice of indoor plants than a dramatic effect of colours and shapes.

Indoor plants can contribute to an improvement in the indoor atmosphere to the benefit of those who live in the house. The plants will. by the nature of their growth. increase the oxygen content of the air and raise the degree of air humidity. so that the air inside the house becomes more comfortable to live in; this is of special significance in modern. well-insulated houses. where the renewal of the air is made more difficult by the use of modern building techniques.

1. **Cyrtomium falcatum**

2 a

2

2. Platycerium bifurcatum
Stag-horn Fern
a. Plant attached to an old log

3. Auracaria excelsa
Norfolk Island Pine

3

4

4. Cyperus alternifolius
Umbrella Plant

**5. Oplismenus imbecilis
"Variegatus"**

5

6
6. Howea belmoreana
Kentia Palm

7. Aglaonema pseudobracteatum
a. Leaf of *A. roebellinii*,
b. Leaf of *A. oblongifolium curtisii*

7 a   7   7 b

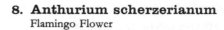

8. Anthurium scherzerianum
Flamingo Flower

9. Anthurium crystallinum

9

10. Dieffenbachia picta
Dumb Cane
a. Plant 1/20th scale

11. Dieffenbachia leopoldii

11

10

10 a

12. **Monstera pertusa**
a. Plant 1/15th scale

12

12 a

13. Spathiphyllum patinii
White Sails

14. Zantedeschia aethiopica
Arum Lily

14

15

15. Rhoeo discolor

16. Tradescantia albiflora
Wandering Jew
a. Plant 1/20th scale

17. Zebrina pendula
a. Plant 1/20th scale

a 16 17

17 a

18. Agapanthus orientalis
African Lily

19 b

19. Aloe variegata
Partridge-breasted Aloe
a. Flowering plant
b. Single non-flowering plant

19 a

20. Chlorophytum comosum variegatum
Spider Plant

21. Dracaena deremensis

22. Dracena marginata

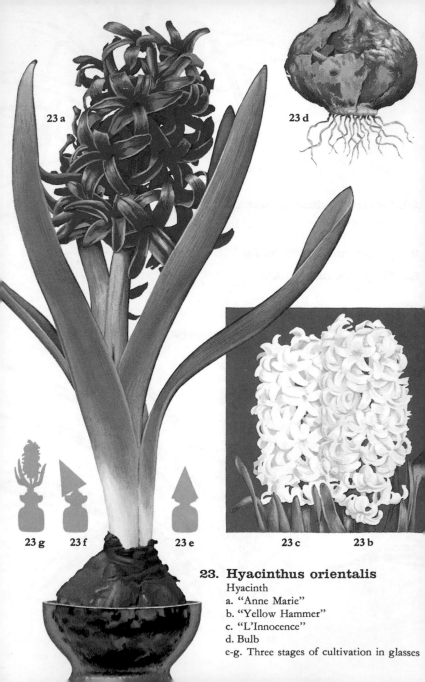

23. Hyacinthus orientalis
Hyacinth
a. "Anne Marie"
b. "Yellow Hammer"
c. "L'Innocence"
d. Bulb
e-g. Three stages of cultivation in glasses

24. Lilium auratum
a. Plant 1/15th scale

24 a

24

25 a

25

25. Sanseveria trifasciata
Mother-in-Law's Tongue
a. *Laurentii* variety

26. Tulipa gesneriana
a. "Brilliant Star"
b. "Bellona"
c. Bulb

27. Tulipa praestans "Fusilier"

28

8. Aechmea fasciata
9. Billbergia windii

30. Nidularium innocentii
a. Plant 1/10th scale

31. Tillandsia cyanea

32. Vriesia splendens

30

30 a

31

32

33. Agave americana
Century Plant
34. Clivia miniata
Kaffir Lily

34

35 a

35. Haemanthus puniceus
a. Showing flower bud

36. Hippeastrum hortorum
Amaryllis
a. Bulb

35

36

36 a

37. Narcissus pseudonarcissus
Daffodil
a. Bulb

38. Narcissus poetaz "Geranium"

37 a

37

38

39. Sprekelia formosissima
Jacobean Lily

39

40. Vallota speciosa
Scarborough Lily
a. Plant 1/19th scale

41. **Cattleya labiata**
Cattleya
a. Mauve variety
b. Flower of white variety

43. Paphiopedilum hybridum
Slipper Orchid

44 a

44

44. Odontoglossum grande
a. Flowers life size

45. Oncidium ornithorhynchum
a. Flowers life size

45 a

45

46. Maranta leuconeura kerchoveana
Prayer Plant
a. Flower life size

46 a

47. Ficus benjamina
a. Plant 1/20th scale

49. Ficus elastica
India Rubber Plant

49

50

50. Ficus pumila
Creeping Fig

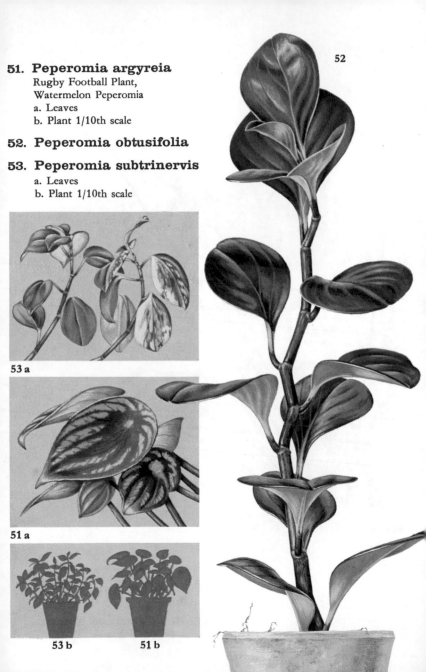

51. Peperomia argyreia
Rugby Football Plant,
Watermelon Peperomia
a. Leaves
b. Plant 1/10th scale

52. Peperomia obtusifolia

53. Peperomia subtrinervis
a. Leaves
b. Plant 1/10th scale

53 a

51 a

53 b   51 b

52

54. Dianthus caryophyllus
Carnation

55. Bougainvillea glabra
a. Plant 1/20th scale

54

55

55 a

56. Argyroderma testiculare
57. Conophytum springbokensis
58. Faucaria tigrina
59. Fenestraria rhopalophylla

62

63. **Mamillaria hidalgensis**

64. **Opuntia phaecantha** (form)
    Prickly Pear

65. **Selenicereus grandiflorus**
    Night-flowering Cereus

64   63

66

66. Rhipsalidopsis rosea
67. Schlumbergera bridgesii
Christmas Cactus

68 a

68. Epiphyllum hybridum
a. White variety
b. Flower of red variety

69. Passiflora coerulea
Passion Flower

68 b

69

70 b

70 a

70. Begonia cheimantha
"Gloire de Lorraine"
(B. socotrana X B. dregei)
a. Red variety
b. Flower of white variety

71. Begonia rex-cultorum

71

72 b

72 c

72 d

72 a

72. Begonia tuberhybrida
a. White variety
b-d. Flowers of other varieties

73. Camellia japonica

74. Pelargonium x domesticum
Regal Pelargonium
(U.S.A. Martha Washington Geranium)

75. Pelargonium x hortorum
Geranium

76. Pelargonium peltatum
Ivy-leaved Geranium

77. Impatiens walleriana
Busy Lizzie

78. Fortunella japonica
Kumquat

79

79. Sparmannia africana
African Hemp

80. Abutilon megatopamicum
Brazilian Abutilon

81. Abutilon striatum thompsonii
Thompson's Abutilon

82. Hibiscus rosa-sinensis
Hibiscus
a. Double-red form
b. Flower of yellow variety

82 b   82 a

83 a

83

83. **Codiaeum variegatum**
Croton
a. Plant 1/20th scale

84. **Euphorbia pulcherrima**
Poinsettia
a. Red variety
b. Pink variety
c. White variety

84 b

84 a   84 c

85

85 a

86

86 a

85. Euphorbia milii
Crown of Thorns
a. Plant 1/10th scale

86. Euphorbia pugniformis
a. Plant 1/10th scale

87 a

87 b

87

88

87. **Bryophyllum daigremontianum**
a-b. Young plantlets

88. **Bryophyllum tubiflorum**

89. **Crassula portulacea**
Jade Plant

90. Crassula falcata
91. Echeveria gibbiflora metallica

92. Echeveria elegans
93. Kalanchoe blossfeldiana

92

91

94

94. **Saxifraga stolonifera**
Mother of Thousands

95. **Pittosporum tobira**

96

96 a

97. Cytisus canariensis
Genista
a. Plant 1/10th scale

97

97 a

98. **Acacia cyanophylla**
a. Plant 1/20th scale

99. **Acacia dealbata decurrens**
Mimosa

99

98 a

98

100. **Fuchsia hybrida**

a. Flower with red sepals and violet corolla
b. Flower of *F. fulgens* hybrid
c. Flower with red sepals and white corolla

100 a   100 b   100 c

101. Punica granatum
Pomegranate
a-b. Flowers and bud, life size

101 a

101 b

101

102. Eucalyptus globulus
Blue Gum
a. Plant 1/10th scale

102 a   102

105

103

105

105 a

103. Fatshedera lizei

104. Hedera canariensis
Canary Island Ivy

105. Hedera helix
Ivy
a. Plant 1/15th scale

104

106. Erica gracilis
Christmas Heather
a. Sprig shown life size

107. Rhododendron simsii
Indian Azalea
a. Pink
b. Red
c. White

106 a

107 a

107 b   -107 c

$(NH_4)_2 SO_4$

108. Cyclamen persicum giganteum
Cyclamen
a. Pink
b. Red flower
c. White flower

109. Primula malacoides
Fairy Primrose
a. Flower, life size

110. Primula kewensis

108 c

108 b

108 a

110

109 a

109

111. Plumbago capensis
Plumbago

111

113. Pharbitis tricolor
Morning Glory

113

114. Brunfelsia calycina
a. Plant 1/10th scale

115. Cestrum purpureum
a. Plant 1/10th scale

115

115 a

116. Datura suaveolens
Angel's Trumpet
a. Plant 1/10th scale

116

116 a

117. Solanum capsicastrum
Christmas Cherry

118. Calceolaria herbeohybrida
Slipper Flower

119

119. Achimenes longiflora

120. Hypocyrta radicans
Clog plant

120

121

121 a

121. **Columnea hybrida**
a. Plant 1/10th scale

122. **Saintpaulia ionantha**
African Violet
a. Pink variety

122

122 a

123. Sinningia speciosa
Gloxinia

124. Streptocarpus hybridus

125. Aphelandra squarrosa
Zebra Plant, Tiger Plant

126. Beloperone guttata
Shrimp Plant

127

127. Fittonia argyroneura
a. Plant 1/5th scale

127 a

128. Thunbergia alata
Black-eyed Susan

129

129 a

129. **Coleus blumei**
Coleus
a. Spray of "Bienvenu"

130. **Plectranthus australis**
a. Plant 1/15th scale

130

130 a

**131. Clerodendrum
speciosissimum**
a. Plant 1/15th scale

131

131 a

132 a

132 b

132. Lantana camara
a. Spray of white-flowered variety
b. Plant 1/10th scale

132

133. **Jasminum polyanthum**
Jasmine
a. Plant 1/10th scale

134. **Allamanda neriifolia**
a. Plant 1/10th scale

133

133 a

134 a   134

135. **Dipladenia sanderii**
a. Plant 1/10th scale

136. **Nerium oleander**
Oleander
a. Plant 1/20th scale
b. Leaf of variegated form

135 a

135

136 b

136 a   136

137

137. Hoya bella

138. Hoya carnosa
Wax Flower

139 a

139

139. Stephanotis floribunda
Bridal Flower
a. Plant 1/20th scale

140. Bouvardia longifolia humboldtii

140

141

141. Coffea arabica
Coffee
a. Part of plant 1/20th scale

141 a

142

142. Gardenia jasminoides
Gardenia
a. Part of plant 1/15th scale

142 a

143. Ixora coccinea
Ixora

144. Manettia inflata
a. Plant 1/10th scale

144 a

144

145

145. Viburnum tinus
Laurustinus

147

146

146. Campanula isophylla alba
Bellflower

147. Campanula isophylla
a. Plant 1/10th scale

147 a

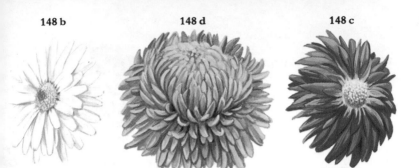

148 b   148 d   148 c

148. Chrysanthemum morifolium hortorum
Chrysanthemum
a. Yellow variety
b. Single white
c. Single bronze
d. Incurved mauve

149. Gazania splendens

150. Senecio cruentus
Cineraria
a. Red variety
b. Blue variety

150 b

150 a

PLANT DESCRIPTIONS AND CULTIVATION

Basic Liquid Fertiliser

As recommended by the author:

3 oz. (100 grams) potassium nitrate
3 oz. (100 grams) calcium phosphate
6 oz. (200 grams) ammonium sulphate

Mix together but keep dry for storage until it is to be used. The powder will dissolve easily in water, and with each application from $\frac{1}{8}$ to $\frac{1}{2}$ oz. per gallon (1–3 grams per litre) should be used, as specified in the individual plant descriptions. This is the fertiliser used throughout the book.

If a proprietary liquid fertiliser is used instead, follow the directions given with it.

Selaginellaceae

Selaginella martensii

Habitat: Hot humid valleys in Mexico.
Growth: Dense fronds with filigree-like blades in delicate light green shades.
Height: 25 cm. (10 in.).
Use: Best in a window facing north or as ground cover in conservatories.
Soil: Light soil, rich in humus, e.g. leaf mould.
Feeding: Weak basic liquid fertiliser, 2 grams per litre ($\frac{1}{2}$ oz. per gallon) every 2

Selaginella martensii

Adiantum cuneatum

weeks (April–October). The roots may be sensitive to excessive artificial fertiliser.
Water: Give plenty of water, and never allow to dry out.
Light: Shade or half-shade, never direct sunlight.
Heat: Summer—fresh, warm air without any draught. Winter—at least 15° C. (60° F.). Rest period October–February.
Syringing: On hot days, but not during the winter.
Re-potting: March, in flat bowls or pans.
Propagation: Divide or layer rooting of shoots in the spring.

Polypodiaceae

Adiantum cuneatum

Maidenhair Fern

Habitat: Tropical rain forests in South America.
Growth: Light and elegant, dark shoots with finely divided light leaves. The leaves have dark sporangia on their undersides.
Use: In warm rooms the ferns are excellent indoor plants. They may be kept in the shade or half-shade all the year, but never put them in the direct sunlight.

Cut stems may be used as green backing for mixed bouquets.

Soil: Humus-rich soil with high peat content. Soilless mixture may be used. The reaction should be slightly acid.

Feeding: Very weak doses of basic liquid fertiliser. Sensitive to nutrient salts, hence only 1 gram per litre ($\frac{1}{4}$ oz. per gallon) per week (March–August).

Water: Plenty of water during the summer growth period, sensitive to drought. Winter, moderate watering. Do not wet the leaves of young plants, but water around the outer edge of the pot or into the base dish.

Light: Best in windows facing north or at a distance from the window. Good decoration in halls, corridors, etc., where there is little daylight.

Heat: Summer, normal temperature; winter, 12–16° C. (55–60° F.).

Air: Moist air March–August during development of new shoots. Dry winter air does no harm.

Re-potting: Early spring.

Propagation: Natural propagation takes place with the aid of minute, almost microscopic, spores which may be sown on damp peat, but this method takes a long time. Division of larger plants best in March.

Asplenium nidus

Asplenium bulbiferum

Habitat: Tropical rain forests.

Growth: Pale, feathery foliage. Along the strongest leaf veins, miniature plants develop on the surfaces of the leaves; these may be detached and planted up in small pots.

Use: Best in special flower windows or warm conservatories. Less suitable as an indoor plant.

Cultivation: As for *Adiantum cuneatum* but requires somewhat higher temperature. Summer, as warm as possible; winter, not below minimum 12° C. (54° F.).

Other species: See below.

Asplenium nidus

Bird's Nest Fern

Growth: Tropical epiphyte (a plant which grows on another). Large leaves undivided around the edges, like a miniature banana leaf. These leaves sprout from a rosette, the centre of which is rather like a bird's nest.

Use and culture: As for *Asplenium bulbiferum.*

Cyrtomium falcatum   (1

Habitat: Eastern Asia.

Growth: Young shoots rolled up like bishops' croziers; older leaves stiff, shiny and leathery (coriaceous). The leaves have dense sporangia on their undersides.

Asplenium bulbiferum

Use: Good indoor plant in shady situation.
Culture: As for *Adiantum cuneatum*, but will stand somewhat lower temperatures.

Nephrolepsis exaltata

Habitat: Tropical America.
Growth: Metre-long, feathery leaves radiating outwards from the central growing point. These leaves may take root at their tips and form new plants, like runners from a strawberry plant.
Use: A good indoor plant in a warm room. The most rewarding of the indoor ferns.
Culture: High room temperature; winter, not below minimum 12° C. (55° F.). Humid air, but no draught or direct sunlight.
Propagation: By runners which will take root.
Varieties: 'Rooseveltii' with single feather-pattern leaves, and 'Whitmannii' with double feather-pattern leaves.

Platycerium bifurcatum (2)

Stag-horn Fern

Habitat: Tropical areas in Africa, Australia and India.
Growth: Epiphyte with poorly developed roots and two kinds of leaves. The large flat plate-like leaves, which entirely cover the roots, are first bright green, then coriaceous and brown. They remain on the plant after fading, and help to form the humus on which—to a considerable extent—it lives. From the growth point between these sterile leaves, long narrow spore-bearing leaves are formed which are shaped like the antlers of a stag or elk, hence the name. Under suitable conditions the fertile leaves can grow a metre (3 ft.) in length; they are covered with whitish scales, and are sensitive to drops of water.
Use: Hanging plants in flower windows

facing north, warm room or shaded winter garden.
Soil: Sphagnum or shredded bark in orchid baskets. The plant can also be tied to a slightly rotten piece of branch or a thick piece of bark. Peat litter, sphagnum or rotted cow-dung may also be packed in among the roots.
Feeding: It is not necessary to feed the plant, but if the basic liquid fertiliser is used, then the proportion of $\frac{1}{4}$ oz. to a gallon is advised, and only feed once every 3 weeks.
Water: The floury leaves will not tolerate drops of water or direct watering. The plant containers or covering leaves must therefore be dipped into a vessel of warm water without moistening the fertile leaves.
Light: As for other types of ferns.
Heat: High room temperature; winter, not below minimum 12° C. (55° F.).
Air: Will stand quite dry room air, but no draught.
Re-potting: Generally unnecessary.

Pteris cretica

Habitat: Mediterranean countries.
Growth: Unevenly divided leaves, with sporangia along the edge of their undersides.
Use: Particularly reliable and straightforward indoor plant.
Culture: Makes no great demands on care and growth conditions. Growth may frequently be so vigorous as to require replanting once or twice a year

Nephrolepsis exaltata

Pteris cretica

in larger pots. Winter temperatures not below minimum 10° C. (50° F.).
Variant: Albo-lineata, with pale stripes on its leaves.

Auracariaceae

Auracaria excelsa (3)

Norfolk Island Pine

Habitat: Norfolk Islands, between Australia and New Zealand, hence its name.
Growth: An evergreen conifer of pyramidal habit, with the branches radiating horizontally in groups of 5 to each tier.
Use: Good indoor plant in a cool, airy and shaded spot. Requires plenty of space on all sides, so that the branches are not deflected.
Soil: Acid loam with peat or pine leaf-mould.
Feeding: 2 grams of ammonium sulphate per litre ($\frac{1}{2}$ oz. per gallon) every three weeks (March–August).
Water: Plenty of water during the summer; must never be allowed to dry out. In winter, the pot soil should be kept slightly damp. Use rainwater or any other soft water. Grows well in plastic pots.
Light: Gentle shade the whole year round. May be allowed to spend the summer out of doors in the shade of

trees. If too strongly shaded during the winter, the bottom leaves turn yellow and fall off.
Heat: Cool the whole year round; winter, best at minimum 14° C. (60° F.).
Air: Gentle breeze when the new shoots come through in the spring. Otherwise, dry indoor air.
Re-potting: Older plants, every 3 years in the spring.
Cutting: Top shoots must not be removed, since if a tier of branches disappears, no replacement is formed.
Propagation: By taking cuttings of top shoots in specialised nurseries, for example in Belgium. When the side shoots are rooted, they will retain their horizontal growth. Propagation impossible indoors.
Pest: Mealy Bug.
NOTE: Arrange for growth in cool, airy and shaded spot, acid soil and rain water. Never allow the pot soil to dry up.

Cyperaceae

Cyperus alternifolius (4)

Umbrella Plant

Habitat: Swampy terrain in Madagascar. Closely related to Papyrus, *Cyperus papyrus*, which was used by the Ancient Egyptians for making paper.
Growth: Stems measuring 30–70 cm. (1–2$\frac{1}{2}$ ft.), ending in a crown of slender leaves radiating outwards like the ribs of a parasol. In the spring, a circle of brownish-green blooms grows above the crown of leaves.
Use: Good indoor plant, which should always stand in water. Growth period March–September.
Soil: Soilless mixture, mixed with ordinary garden soil and sand. pH 7. Leaf tips turn brown in very acid or very alkaline soil.
Feeding: 2 grams per litre ($\frac{1}{4}$ oz. per gallon) every week (April–August).
Water: Grows well in a vessel of water,

and must in any case always have plenty of water. Avoid limey tap water or neutralise it with 1 gram of ammonium sulphate per litre ($\frac{1}{4}$ oz. per gallon). The water in the base dish or pot should not be changed but replenished as it is used or evaporates. Remember to keep water in the base dish throughout the summer.
Light: Full sunlight or moderate shade, i.e. in windows facing in any direction.
Heat: Usual room temperature; winter, not below minimum 10° C. (50° F.).
Air: Damp air, frequent spraying in dry indoor air.
Re-potting: March–July.
Cutting: Withered leaf shoots should be removed from the base. Older plants may be cut down completely.
Propagation: By division of older plants. Leaf cuttings can be taken by cutting off a leaf with a 1-cm. ($\frac{1}{4}$-in.) stem, and allowing this to float on the surface of a dish filled with water at a minimum temperature of 20° C. (70° F.). Small plants will develop in the axils, and can be planted in small pots with damp sand, where they will rapidly strike roots.

Scirpus cernuus

Habitat: Swamp terrain in the East Indies.
Growth: Grassy marsh plant with thick

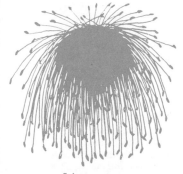

Scirpus cernuus

tussocks of dark, shiny triangular straws which hang out over the edges of the pots, giving the impression of a wig. During the summer, small brownish-green flowers appear at the tips of the straws.
Use: Good indoor plant which, as for *Cyperus alternifolius*, should stand in water. Grows best in plastic pots with water in base dishes.
Soil: Soilless mixture.
Feeding: 2 grams per litre ($\frac{3}{4}$ oz. per gallon) every 2 weeks (March–September).
Water: There should always be water in the base dish, preferably rainwater or some other lime-free water.
Light: Not direct sunlight.
Heat: Normal room temperature.
Air: The leaves acquire brown tips in dry indoor air, thus frequent spraying is necessary.
Re-potting: February. The innermost shoots grow yellow on older plants; rejuvenate by division and by cutting out of withered shoots.
Propagation: By division.
Pest: Red spider mite.

Gramineae

Oplismenus imbecilis 'Variegatus' (5)

Habitat: Tropics.
Growth: Up to 50 cm. (20 in.) in length, hanging shoots with narrow leaves striped longitudinally with green, pink or white. Superficial appearance similar to *Tradescantia*. Only the older, exhausted plants produce flowers, which are not particularly decorative.
Use: Good, undemanding plants in warm rooms. Young plants are most attractive, and for this reason cuttings should be taken from the top shoots each year and the old plants discarded.
Soil: Humus-rich loam or soilless mixture.
Feeding: 3 grams per litre (1 oz. per gallon) every week (March–October),

otherwise the leaf tips become scorched and turn yellow and discoloured. Avoid wetting the leaves when feeding.

Water: Plenty of water in the summer and spring; moderate amounts in winter.

Light: Well-lit spot for growth, especially during the winter.

Heat: Normal room temperature; winter, not below minimum 10° C. (50° F.).

Air: Grows well in dry, indoor air. During propagation by grafting, needs more humid air.

Re-potting: Not usually worth while. Plants may instead be rejuvenated by putting cuttings of top shoots in March straight into flower-pots filled with soilless mixture mixed with sand, in a sealed atmosphere under glass or a plastic hood.

Pests: Greenfly, red spider mite.

Pandanaceae

Pandanus veitchii

Screw Pine

Habitat: Polynesia.

Growth: Excellent decorative plant, which has the appearance of a palm tree without a trunk. The narrow, pointed, metre-length (3-ft.) leaves are dark green with white edges. The individual leaves appear in the rosette in screw-thread or spiral formation around the plant's central axis, while the leaf tips have pointed thorns. Older plants develop buttress-roots, which 'jack up' the plant from the earth, so that it has 'stilts' to stand upon. Small plants often develop on the aerial roots.

Use: Undemanding indoor plant, which, however, may grow too big under normal conditions. Older specimens may be discarded and replaced with small, more decorative, new plants.

Soil: Soilless mixture.

Feeding: 3 grams per litre (1 oz. per gallon) every 2 weeks (March–October).

Water: Plenty of water in spring and summer; moderate amounts in winter.

Light: Best in the half-shade. Never in windows facing south.

Heat: Growth period, summer at minimum 20–25° C. (70–80° F.). Winter, slightly cooler. Growth ceases at temperatures below minimum 15° C. (60° F.).

Air: Dry indoor air with spraying during summer.

Re-potting: March; pots should not be too small.

Propagation: Cut side shoots, which often form roots while they are on the parent plant.

NOTE: Often grows too big for an indoor plant. Best in a conservatory. Take care with the pointed thorns.

Other species: See below.

Pandanus sanderi

Habitat: Solomon Islands.

Growth: Dark green leaves with yellow stripes.

Use and culture: As for *Pandanus veitchii.*

Pandanus utilis

Habitat: Madagascar.

Growth: Bluish-green leaves with reddish-brown thorns at the edges.

Use and culture: As for *Pandanus veitchii.*

Pandanus veitchii

Palmae

Palms

Habitat: The palm family includes over 1000 tropical and sub-tropical varieties from all parts of the world.

Growth: Palms are elegant foliage-plants, often having elegantly dissected leaves with or without trunks.

Use: Only the smaller varieties are suitable as indoor plants. Older plants, on the other hand, often become too large for indoor culture and must be moved to a conservatory or greenhouse. Seldom flower in indoor culture. Palms grow the whole year round without any real rest period, and for this reason the culture requirements are more or less the same all the year, regulated according to quantity of light and temperature. All palms have certain cultural requirements in common, which are described below; any special cultural requirements are mentioned with the individual species.

Soil: Soilless mixture or well-drained humus soil. pH 5–6·5 (i.e. slightly acid).

Feeding: 2 grams per litre ($\frac{1}{4}$ oz. per gallon) every week (March–October), but only after prior watering.

Water: Plenty of water during the summer, otherwise moderate quantities. The soil balls must never be allowed to dry out completely.

Light: Windows facing east or west; no direct sunlight.

Heat: Normal room temperature. Minimum temperature 18°C. (65°F.) for the types requiring most heat; for the remainder, minimum 15°C. (60°F.).

Air: Frequent syringing to increase air humidity.

Re-potting: Every spring, February–March. Older plants, on the other hand, every two or three years. Use deep, narrow pots, so that the aerial roots are not too high. Planting should be very firm; ram the soil in carefully around the edges.

Propagation: Seeding may be successful indoors. Soil temperature approximate minimum 30°C. (85°F.). The seeds may remain in the soil for several months before the shoots become visible.

Pests: Scale insects, mealy bug, red spider mites and thrips, especially when plants are placed in warm or sunlit positions.

Varieties: See below.

Chamaedorea elegans (*syn* Neanthe bella)

Habitat: Mexico.

Growth: Hardy dwarf palm with lobed leaves, having 20-cm. (7-in.)-long small leaves. The stem, which develops over the years, is of the thickness of a finger, smooth, with bracts behind the leaves, which later fall away. Even small plants in 10-cm. (3$\frac{1}{2}$-in.) pots form rather insignificant green inflorescences and subsequently exciting, colourful fruit clusters.

Special cultural requirements: A lot of water, also in base dish. High temperature: winter, not below minimum 12°C. (55°F.). For other requirements, see under *Palms.*

Chamaerops humilis

Habitat: Mediterranean countries. Only wild palm in Europe.

Chamaerops humilis

Microcoelum weddelianum

Growth: Stems grow up to a metre (3 ft.) in height, developing first in older plants. The leaves are fan-shaped, with spiny stems.
Special cultural requirements: May be left to spend the summer on a balcony, terrace, or in a patio. Minimum temperature in winter 5° C. (40° F.). In a well-lit place. Other cultural requirements, see under *Palms.*

Microcoelum weddelianum (*syn* Cocos weddelliana)
Known in the United States as Microcoelum mortianum

Habitat: Brazil.
Growth: Smallest, but most decorative of all indoor palms. Has elegant, feather-like leaves. Sold as small plants, and can only be kept in a room for a few years.
Special cultural requirements: Plenty of water, best with permanent water in a base dish. High wintering temperature, at least 18° C. (65° F.). Other cultural requirements, see under *Palms.*

Howea belmoreana   (6)
Kentia Palm
Habitat: Howe Islands in the Pacific, the capital of which is called Kentia, hence also the name *Kentia belmoreana.*
Growth: Very broad and sturdy lobed leaves with wide pendulous leaflets.

Special cultural requirements: Imposes no great demands, but should not be exposed to too harsh sunlight. Best winter temperature, minimum 14–18° C. (55–65° F.). For other cultural requirements, see under *Palms.*

Phoenix canariensis
Habitat: Canary Islands.
Growth: Strong-growing plant, with large, feather-like leaves.
Special cultural requirements: Good tub plant to be placed out of doors in the sun during summer. Winter cool temperature, but not below minimum 5° C. (40° F.). For other cultural requirements, see under *Palms.*

Phoenix dactylifera
Date Palm
Habitat: Tropics.
Growth: Very vigorous grower with stiff, prickly leaves. After 10–15 years it becomes too big as an indoor plant but suitable for a conservatory.
Cultural requirements: See under *Palms.*
Propagation: May be propagated by seeding in ordinary moist soil. For the first year, the palm consists only of a single grass-like leaf.

Phoenix dactylifera

Phoenix roebelinii

Habitat: East Indies.
Growth: Sturdy, undemanding indoor plant with slow growth.
Special cultural requirements:
Minimum temperature in winter 15°C. (60°F.). For other cultural requirements, see under *Palms*.

Araceae

Aglaonema pseudobracteatum   (7)

Habitat: Malaya.
Growth: Foliage plant with pointed, oval leaves, with white central vein and white and yellow markings. Height 40 cm. (16 in.). Flowers have no ornamental value. More durable than *Dieffenbachia*, which has a tendency to shed its lower leaves in indoor culture.
Use: Quite a demanding indoor plant. Will not be squeezed in between other plants, and does not take kindly to being moved. Only lasts a few years in indoor culture.
Soil: Light humus soil mixed with sand, or possibly soilless mixture. The roots lie close to the surface of the soil, and it must therefore be planted in wide, flat pans.
Feeding: 2 grams per litre ($\frac{3}{4}$ oz. per gallon) every 2 weeks (February–July).
Water: Always keep the soil moist; does not stand drying out.
Light: Shade, never direct sunlight. Thrives well in dark entrance halls or staircases. Best in windows facing east, west or north.
Heat: Likes a warm spot. In a shaded position, the winter temperature can be as low as 15°C. (60°F.) minimum, but otherwise warmer.
Air: Stands up to dry air. In very warm atmospheres, however, needs frequent syringing.
Re-potting: February, in pans rather than pots.
Pests: Mealy bug, red spider mite.
Other species: See below.

Aglaonema costatum

Growth: Pointed, oval leaves, with white central vein and white spots. Height 20 cm. (8 in.).
Use and culture: As for *Aglaonema pseudobracteatum.*

Aglaonema modestum

Growth: Unvariegated green leaves. Height 30 cm. (1 ft.).
Use and culture: As for *Aglaonema pseudobracteatum.*

Aglaonema roebelinii

Growth: Broad, oval leaves, with conspicuous silver-grey markings on the otherwise dark green surface of the leaf. Height 40 cm. (16 in.).
Use and culture: As for *Aglaonema pseudobracteatum.*

Aglaonema oblongifolium curtisii

Growth: Narrow, oval-pointed dark green leaves with silvery side veins. Height 40 cm. (16 in.). The sturdiest of the *Aglaonema* varieties.
Use and culture: As for *Aglaonema pseudobracteatum.*

Anthurium scherzerianum   (8)

Flamingo Flower

Habitat: Guatemala.
Growth: The leaf and flower stems shoot forth from the necks of the roots at the surface of the soil. The leaves are narrow and dark green in colour, and have long stems. The small yellow flowers are gathered into a dense spike or spadix, reminiscent of a pig's tail; this spike is surrounded by a scarlet, pale red or white spathe, which persists for several months.
Use: Durable and decorative indoor plant, which has a preference for warm,

humid air but thrives surprisingly well in an ordinary room atmosphere.

Soil: Very light, porous mixture, e.g. soilless mixture and sand. Bracken peat and leaf mould with charcoal added is also a good mixture.

Feeding: 6 grams per litre (2 oz. per gallon) every 3 weeks (February–December), but apply only when the soil ball is already moist. Roots are sensitive to too high a concentration of salts in the soil; it will therefore be an advantage to use an organic fertiliser (such as cowdung) alternately with artificial fertiliser.

Water: The light porous mixture dries out quickly and, since the plant is damaged if allowed to dry out even once, frequent watering is an unbreakable rule. The best method is to dip the entire pot into lukewarm water. Rainwater is to be preferred.

Light: Half or full shade. Will not tolerate direct sunlight.

Heat: Winter not below a minimum 15° C. (60° F.).

Air: Moist air with frequent syringing.

Re-potting: Early spring, when the necks of the roots have pushed themselves up over the surface of the soil, in wide, flat pots with plenty of room for the roots. Never plant too deeply.

Diseases: Brown edges on the leaves when the soil or air is too dry, and the light too harsh. Avoid calcium deposits on leaves when watering.

Other species: See below.

Anthurium crystallinum (9)

Habitat: Peru.

Growth: Handsome foliage plant with very large, velvety, olive-green leaves having silvery-white veins.

Use: Best in very warm greenhouse or conservatory. Uncertain in room culture.

Culture: Similar to *Anthurium scherzerianum*, but requires higher temperatures and higher degree of air humidity.

Dieffenbachia picta (10)
Dumb Cane

Habitat: Tropical America.

Growth: Sturdy, erect trunk with clear green leaves on long stems with dots and blotches in white, pale yellow and pale green. Cultivated as a young plant and discarded when the bottom leaves are shed, its value as an ornamental plant is thus debatable.

Use: Best in a warm greenhouse, but also good in a room after careful hardening off. Thrives for a time in deep shade. Requires a lot of space.

Soil: Soilless mixture or light leaf mould with peat added.

Feeding: 3 grams per litre (1 oz. per gallon) every week (March–October).

Water: Should be kept moist all the year round. Will not stand drying out.

Light: Never direct sunlight. Thrives in shady rooms, halls or staircases.

Heat: Poor growth if temperature falls below minimum 15° C. (60° F.) during winter.

Air: Frequent spraying, especially in summer.

Re-potting: Every spring, in spacious pots.

Propagation: By cuttings in a greenhouse in an enclosed atmosphere, with bottom heat.

Pests: Mealy bug, red spider mite, especially when the growing point is too brightly lit.

NOTE: The sap in the leaves and stems is poisonous.

Other varieties: There are many hybrids between this and other species with a great variation in the distribution of colours in the leaves. See also below.

Dieffenbachia leopoldii (11)

Growth: Very popular *Dieffenbachia* species with plain green leaves.

Use and culture: As for *Dieffenbachia picta*.

Monstera deliciosa (12)

Habitat: Tropical swamps in Mexico.

Growth: Sturdy climbing plant; the large shield-like leaves have lobed incisions and holes. From the stems, large bunches of hanging aerial roots are formed. Older plants may, under favourable conditions in conservatories or hothouses, develop large, calla-like inflorescences with white spathes. Later, aromatic edible fruits appear, which have a taste similar to that of a pineapple.

Use: Decorative room plant, requiring a lot of space. Suitable for trellising to walls, doorways and large windows.

Soil: Soilless mixture, or garden soil with added peat. pH 6·5.

Feeding: 3 grams per litre (1 oz. per gallon) every week (March–October). Fertiliser should only be applied to moist soil.

Water: Plenty in the summer, moderate amount in the winter.

Light: Shade or half-shade. In brightly lit positions, the leaves acquire brown spots and edges.

Heat: Normal room temperature, but not less than 12° C. (55° F.).

Air: Syringe during growth. Will stand up to very good centrally heated air.

Re-potting: Every 3 or 4 years.

Propagation: By cutting top shoots with the aerial roots attached. They should be planted in equal parts of soilless mixture and sand, and must be kept moist and warm.

Varieties: borsigiana (but correctly *Monstera pertusa*), which has smaller leaves and more aerial roots than the type, and grows more rapidly and vigorously. Can also be used in smaller rooms. This is the variety illustrated.

NOTE: Aerial roots, which—like ordinary roots—serve as ducts for transmitting water and nourishment, must not be removed. They can be trained down into a base dish which is permanently filled with water in order to facilitate the plant's growth. Deficiency of 'window holes' in the leaves is the result of too little water and nourishment and too dark a growth position.

Philodendron scandens

Sweetheart Vine

Habitat: West Indies.

Growth: Vigorous climbing plant (liana) with pointed, heart-shaped leaves which —while very small on young plants— grow to lengths of 30 cm. (1 ft.) on older specimens. New leaves are reddish-brown and almost transparent.

Use: Well suited as climbing plants on trellises or walls or as a hanging-basket plant, also as a ground covering in conservatories. An amusing method of culture is to allow the plant to grow up a stick enveloped in moist moss or sphagnum. Good for shady situations. One of our most attractive and hardiest indoor plants.

Soil: Soilless mixture.

Feeding: 3 grams per litre (1 oz. per gallon) every week (March–September).

Water: Summer, plentiful; winter, moderate.

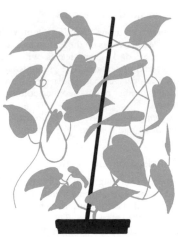

Philodendron scandens

Philodendron erubescens

Light: Easily satisfied, does not stand direct sunshine.

Heat: Normal room temperature; not less than 12°C. (55°F.). Avoid violent fluctuations of temperature.

Air: Syringing when room temperature is high.

Re-potting: Spring, in pots which must not be too large.

Propagation: By cuttings with aerial roots, as for *Monstera deliciosa.*

Other species: See below.

Philodendron erubescens

Growth: Vigorous climbing plant with dark red markings on the leaf stems, and glistening dark green leaves with red edges and undersides. The young leaves are a coppery colour. Older plants produce a number of dark, copper-coloured flowers.

Use and culture: As for *Philodendron scandens,* and is as easily satisfied.

Philodendron ilsemannii

Growth: Climbing plant with variegated leaves and slow-growing stems. The lancet-shaped dark green leaves have irregular white markings. The variegated patterns disappear in poor light conditions.

Use and culture: As for *Philodendron scandens.* Considerably less hardy.

Philodendron bipinnatifidum

Growth: Vigorous foliage plant with no climbing stems. The body of the leaf is 50 cm. (20 in.) long and feathered; the leaf stems are also 50 cm. (20 in.) long, and hollow. The leaves sprout from a central growing point.

Use: Requires a lot of space; therefore best in a conservatory.

Culture: As for *Philodendron scandens.*

Philodendron melanochrysum (*this is the juvenile form of* P. andreanum)

Growth: The most decorative of the Philodendron species. The leaves, shaped like arrow shafts hanging vertically and overlapping, are dark green with shades of copper and pale yellow veins. They grow to 80 cm. (32 in.). In electric light the leaves look as if they are covered with gold dust.

Use and culture: As for *Philodendron scandens,* but needs higher temperatures—not below 18°C. (65°F.) minimum—and greater air humidity with frequent syringing and more water.

Philodendron melanochrysum

Sauromatum venosum (guttatum)

Monarch of the East

Habitat: East Indies.

Growth: Odd plant with a large tuber, from which first the flower and later the leaves emerge, without culture in soil or water being necessary. The flower is surrounded by an olive-green spathe with purplish-brown markings, and when fully developed gives off a disgusting carrion smell. The leaves are deeply cut and very decorative.

Use: In the early spring, the dry tuber is placed in a warm, dry spot without direct sunlight. Flowering period, February–March. After this the tuber is potted and the plant watered and looked after in the normal way, while the leaves mature. In October the top withers away again. May be put out of doors for the summer but must be taken in before the first night frost. To be kept dry throughout the winter at minimum 10° C. (50° F.).

Soil: Light loam with sand added.

Feeding: 5 grams per litre (1¾ oz. per gallon) every week during growth, until leaves begin to wither.

Water: Plentiful in summer, to be kept dry from October.

Light: Half-shade.

Scindapsus aureus

Heat: Normal room temperature; winter not less than minimum 10° C. (50° F.).

Air: Dry indoor air during flowering. During leaf period, frequent syringing.

Re-potting: Potting after flowering is finished. The tuber is covered with 3 cm. (1¼ in.) of soil.

NOTE: The smell of the withering flower is particularly unpleasant.

Scindapsus aureus

Habitat: East Indies, New Guinea and the Solomon Islands.

Growth: Hanging or climbing plant with longish, symmetrical, fresh green leaves with yellow patterns. The young shoots and leaf stems are yellowish.

Use: Very suitable as a hanging or climbing plant in very shaded situations.

Soil: Light humus soil or standard potting mixture.

Feeding: 3 grams per litre (1 oz. per gallon) every week (March–October).

Water: Soil should be evenly moist in

Sauromatum venosum

summer but never thoroughly wet. Winter, better too dry than too damp.

Light: Imposes no great demands. At high room temperatures, however, during winter, the growth position should be as well-lit as possible.

Heat: Normal room temperature during winter; not less than minimum 15°C. (60°F.).

Air: Frequent sprinkling during summer.

Re-potting: February–May, when growth begins.

Propagation: Cuttings from sections of stems with aerial roots are potted in sand and sphagnum. Keep close until roots have begun to develop.

Other species: See below.

Scindapsus pictus

Growth: Heart-shaped dark green leaves with small silver markings.

Use and culture: As for *Scindapsus aureus.*

Variant: argyraeus, with black-green leaves having silvery-white markings and edges. Well suited for trellising against as dark as possible a background, which may set off the characteristic leaves. Requires more warmth and greater air humidity than the type.

Spathiphyllum patinii (*syn* kochii, wallisii *of nurserymen*) (13)

White Sails

Habitat: Tropical America.

Growth: Smooth, dark green leaves on long stems, from a horizontal root stock. The spadix-shaped inflorescence is yellowish-white, the open spathe pure white. After flowering has finished, the seed cluster and enveloping leaf changes to green. Long-lasting flowers in spring or early summer (often has a second flowering in the autumn).

Use: Sturdy indoor plant in a very dark room. Decorative as a fresh foliage plant outside the flowering season.

Soil: Soilless mixture.

Feeding: 2 grams per litre ($\frac{3}{4}$ oz. per gallon) every 2 weeks (March–September), but only on to damp soil. Too much fertiliser produces brown leaf tips.

Water: Summer, constant soil moisture; winter, moderate watering.

Light: Very easily satisfied; very suitable for windows facing north.

Heat: Normal room temperature; winter not less than minimum 15°C. (60°F.).

Air: Tolerates dry room air.

Re-potting: February–March.

Propagation: By division during re-potting.

Diseases: One of the healthiest indoor plants.

Syngonium auritum

Habitat: Tropical America.

Growth: Vigorous climbing plant with dark green 3- or 5-fingered leaves having spear-shaped lobes.

Use: Easily cultivated climbing plants for trellises or moss-covered rods. Good in the shade, in rooms which are not too cool.

Soil: Soilless mixture.

Feeding: 3 grams per litre (1 oz. per gallon) every week (March–September).

Water: Must not be allowed to dry out. Evenly moist soil is preferable.

Light: Half-shade or full shade, not direct sunlight.

Heat: Normal room temperature; winter, not less than minimum 15°C. (60°F.).

Air: Thrives in very dry room air.

Re-potting: Should be transplanted every year in February so that growth should not be retarded.

Propagation: By taking cuttings of stalk sections together with the aerial roots.

Other species: See below.

Syngonium auritum

Syngonium podophyllum

Goosefoot Plant

Growth: Leaves divided into 5 or 8 sections. Of particular interest is the *albolineatum* form which has velvet green leaves with white stripes along the central and side veins ('Emerald Gem' of nurserymen).

Use and culture: As for *Syngonium auritum*. (Sometimes sold under the name *Nephthytis*.)

Zantedeschia aethiopica (14)

Arum Lily

Habitat: Marshes in South Africa. Often found in the tropics as a luxuriant weed plant in ditches and swamps.

Growth: Perennial, with fleshy tubers and arrowhead-shaped leaves on succulent stalks which may grow up to a metre (3 ft.) in height. From January to April the flower stalks sprout forth with fragrant yellow flower heads surrounded by a cornet-shaped white spathe.

Use: Decorative room plant which requires a great deal of space, and plenty of water during the growth period from July to April. Must be kept absolutely dry during the resting period which is generally from May to June, but sometimes the plants continue growing until June. May be taken from its pot and planted out in a garden in July once the top has almost withered. Potting in October.

Soil: Soilless mixture.

Feeding: 4 grams per litre ($1\frac{1}{4}$ oz. per gallon) every week during growth period (July–November).

Water: Bog plant which requires plenty of water; a good method is to have permanent water in a base dish. Only during the resting period (May–June) can water be omitted altogether, so that the pot soil can thoroughly dry out.

Light: Tolerates a great deal of light, but the pot with the soil ball must be shielded from direct sunlight.

Heat: Summer, in a garden or on a balcony at normal temperatures. From October to New Year, best at minimum 10° C. (50° F.), subsequently at minimum 15° C. (60° F.) so as to assist flowering.

Air: Humid air with frequent syringing on hot days outside the resting period.

Re-potting: Pot up divided plants in large pots in October after spending the summer out of doors.

Propagation: By division of old plants, also in October.

Diseases: Brown edges on leaves when plants are fed while soil is dry.

Pests: Red spider mite when kept in too light or too dry a location.

Other species: See below.

Zantedeschia elliottiana

Growth: Green leaves with silvery-grey markings. Clear golden-yellow flowers.

Use and culture: As for *Zantedeschia aethiopica*, but needs somewhat higher temperature after New Year (minimum 18° C. (65° F.)) in order to flower.

Zantedeschia elliottiana

Commelinaceae

Rhoeo discolor (*syn* spathacea) (15)

Habitat: Central America.
Growth: Stems up to 30 cm. (1 ft.) high, with lance-shaped leaves arranged in a rosette with olive-green top surfaces and blue-violet undersides. Reminiscent of *Dracaena* and *Bromelia*. The white flowers nestle in the axils, hidden in the cradle-like greenish-violet bracts, from which they just peep out during the short-lived flowering period. In America this is known as 'Moses in the Cradle'.
Use: Good foliage plant for windows facing west or east, where the atmosphere is warm and humid in summer and warm and dry in winter. Most attractive as a single plant.
Soil: Soilless mixture, or loam mixed with sand.
Feeding: 2 grams per litre ($\frac{3}{4}$ oz. per gallon) every 2 weeks (March–September).
Water: Summer, constant moisture in the soil; winter, dry so that the shoots do not rot on the surface of the soil.
Light: Shaded situation for the summer, lighter spot for winter.
Heat: Summer, normal room temperature; winter, not less than minimum 15° C. (60° F.).

Air: The leaves roll up in dry air. Spray well in summer.
Re-potting: March–June in large pots, in which the plants will rapidly grow larger.
Propagation: By taking cuttings of side shoots in early spring.
Variant: vittata, which has yellow and white longitudinal stripes on the leaves. Slower growth and more heat and light required in winter than for the type.

Tradescantia albiflora (16)

Wandering Jew

Habitat: Tropical America.
Growth: Creeping and hanging growth, with succulent plain green leaves and shoots. Flowers are in bloom from early summer to autumn. They are white, and only open for a few hours.
Use: Excellent hanging plant in windows which are not too bright. Indifferent to fluctuations in temperature and thrives at temperatures from minimum 10–25° C. (50–80° F.). May be cultivated as a 'water plant' with cut runners in water. Good for cultivation in plastic pots.
Soil: Soilless mixture.
Feeding: 3 grams per litre (1 oz. per gallon) every 2 weeks (March–September). When too much nourishment is given, the colours of the leaves fade on the more gaily-coloured varieties.
Water: The soil must always be kept damp, especially during summer.
Light: Half-shade or full shade, ever full sunlight.
Heat: Normal room temperature; winter, not less than minimum 10° C. (50° F.) however.
Air: Likes humid air, but thrives well in dry indoor air as long as it is given plenty of water.
Re-potting: Older plants grow spindly and unattractive, and should therefore be discarded in favour of one-year-old plants.
Propagation: By cuttings of top shoots in the spring, either in water followed by

potting after the formation of roots, or directly into damp soilless mixture in small pots with several cuttings in each.
Pest: Greenfly.
Variant: aureovittata with irregular yellow stripes on the leaves.
Other species: See below.

Tradescantia blossfeldiana

Growth: Covered with thick, white fur. The leathery leaves are green on their upper sides and red on their undersides. The flowers are pink.
Use and culture: As for *Tradescantia albiflora.*

Tradescantia fluminensis

Growth: Reddish violet stems, green leaves with violet undersides, and white flowers in great profusion.
Use and culture: As for *Tradescantia albiflora.*
Variety: albovittata with white-striped leaves.

Tradescantia navicularis

Growth: Thick leaves. Grows more slowly than the other *Tradescantia* varieties.
Use and culture: As for *Tradescantia albiflora.* Must be kept cool and in the light during winter. Minimum temperature 10° C. (50° F.).

Zebrina pendula (17)

Habitat: Central America and Mexico.
Growth: Fast-growing hanging plant, which can only be distinguished from *Tradescantia* by obscure botanical differences. The leaves are dark green with two silvery-white stripes on the upper sides. The purplish-pink flowers emerge in the early spring.
Use: Hanging plant for windows facing east or west. Even growth all the year round with no real resting period.

Soil: Standard potting mixture.
Feeding: 3 grams per litre (1 oz. per gallon) every 2 weeks (March–October). Too much nitrogen will cause the colours to fade.
Water: Summer, plenty; winter, moderate.
Light: Half or full shade; winter somewhat lighter.
Heat: Normal room temperature; winter, not below minimum 10° C. (50° F.).
Air: Preferably humid air. The leaves roll up in very dry room air.
Re-potting: Not advisable. Older plants are unattractive and should be replaced by younger ones.
Propagation: Remove top shoots in the spring and plant them, several together in each pot, in soilless compost mixed with sand. Plastic pots are very suitable.
Pests: Greenfly, snails and slugs.
Variety: quadricolor, in which the leaves, in addition to the other colours, have white and light red stripes on their upper sides.

Liliaceae

Agapanthus orientalis (18)

African Lily

Habitat: South Africa.
Growth: Vigorous plant growing to 75 cm. (2½ ft.) long, narrow leaves and pretty blue flowers on long stems. Flowers throughout the summer.
Use: Requires a lot of space. Very suitable as a tub plant in a patio, on a terrace or a balcony. To be kept dry and cool but frost-free during winter in a cellar or unheated conservatory. To assist flowering, the plant must be kept completely dry from November to the beginning of May.
Soil: Rich compost with bonemeal added. Good drainage.
Feeding: 3 grams per litre (1 oz. per gallon) every week (May–July).
Water: Must be kept well watered from May to October. After that, the water

must be given sparingly and the plant kept completely dry from November to May.

Light: Well-lit situation; may be in full sunlight. Winter, as close to daylight as possible.

Heat: Summer, normal temperature; winter, minimum 2–8° C. (38–45° F.). Will not stand frost.

Air: Spray on hot summer days.

Re-potting: See Propagation.

Propagation: Every 3 or 4 years the older plants should be divided, preferably in April. Frequent disturbance will discourage flowering. Administer basic feeding with bonemeal (Animix) on re-potting.

Pest: Greenfly.

Aloe arborescens

Habitat: South Africa.

Growth: Succulent, with upright stems and thick fleshy leaves having prickly edges. Large clusters of orange-red bell-shaped flowers.

Use: Ideal indoor plant, the growth period of which comes, in contrast to that of many other indoor plants, in the winter-time, while flowering takes place from March to July.

Aloe arborescens

Soil: Loam and sand with good drainage at the base of the pot.

Feeding: 3 grams per litre (1 oz. per gallon) every 2 weeks (February–December).

Water: Moderate watering during growth period in winter and spring, while the plant is kept relatively dry during the summer and during its resting period.

Light: Full sunlight.

Heat: Normal room temperature; summer, as cool as possible. Minimum temperature 10° C. (50° F.).

Air: Thrives best in dry air, thus well suited for centrally heated rooms. Avoid excessive moisture on the plant, which might cause the stem to rot.

Re-potting: At intervals of several years in pots which are not too large, after flowering has ceased in July–August.

Propagation: By side shoots or leaf cuttings, the cut surface of which must be allowed to dry before they are planted in soil with a generous amount of sand added.

Diseases: Tendency to rot if watered too heavily or if the degree of air humidity is too high.

Other species: See below.

Aloe variegata   (19)

Partridge-breasted Aloe

Growth: Triangular leaves with white markings, arranged in a distinct cross pattern, and a white prickly edge. The flowers are large and orange-red with drops of pleasant-tasting nectar.

Use and culture: As for *Aloe arborescens*.

NOTE: Will not tolerate water in the rosette.

Asparagus sprengeri

Habitat: Natal.

Growth: Thin, trailing branches with narrow needle-like leaves. Older plants develop thorns. The plant must be constantly rejuvenated by cutting away old shoots.

Use: Good plant for hanging bowls, even under poor conditions. Thrives in undrained flower-pots. Will stand either warm or cold wintering, and omission of resting period which is October–March. In commercial nurseries, this and—even more—the following species are extensively used as greenery for bouquets of flowers.

Soil: Soilless compost mixture or humus-rich loam with pH 6·5.

Feeding: 5 grams per litre ($1\frac{1}{2}$ oz. per gallon) every week (March–August).

Water: During growth period, plenty of water, but must be kept drier during the winter. The swollen tubers protect it from drying out.

Light: Light, sunny place. Does not like shade or dark rooms, which cause small and discoloured leaves.

Heat: Summer, normal room temperature; winter, minimum 12–20° C. (50–70° F.) in a well-lit growing position.

Air: When the resting period ends in February the plant likes humid air with frequent sprinkling. Otherwise dry room air.

Re-potting: February, in large pots, as the roots require a lot of space.

Propagation: By division of old plants, otherwise by seed.

Pests: Greenfly, with too much heat in the spring. Do not spray with nicotine, which scorches the plant, but use Lindasect or something similar.

Diseases: Small leaves are shed when there is a lack of light or when the temperature fluctuates too sharply.

Other species: See below.

Asparagus plumosus

Asparagus Fern

Growth: Pretty indoor plant with very finely divided foliage. The variety *compactus* can be used as a house plant. Flowers readily and grows pretty red

Asparagus plumosus

berries.* Produces fresh shoots whenever pruned. Best plant for cut greenery.

Use and culture: As for *Asparagus sprengeri,* but somewhat more difficult indoors since it will not tolerate warm, dry air during the winter. Prefers cool, humid air and slight shade.

Aspidistra elatior

Habitat: Southern Japan.

Growth: Broad, lancet-shaped leaves sprout like gigantic Lily of the Valley leaves from the thick, fleshy root stocks. Unattractive, brownish-violet flowers right on the surface of the soil.

Use: One of our most easily satisfied indoor plants, which thrives even in the darkest corner of the room. Ideal for stairways and as a 'restaurant plant'.

Soil: Soilless mixture.

Feeding: In summer, 3 grams per litre (1 oz. per gallon) every 2 weeks, but only on moist soil.

Water: Summer, moderate watering; winter, less.

Light: Will stand deep shade, but better growth in a lighter place in a window facing north, north-west or north-east.

* But the plant is dioecious and plants of both sexes are necessary.

Aspidistra elatior

Heat: Normal room temperature.
Air: Will stand dry room air, but much better growth in humid air.
Re-potting: Every 2 or 3 years in pots which are not too large.
Propagation: By division on re-potting. Root stocks must be cut through with a sharp knife, so that there are 2–3 leaves on each rhizome.
Pest: Snails or slugs on new leaves.

Chlorophytum comosum variegatum (20)

Spider Plant

Habitat: South Africa.
Growth: The name Spider Plant refers to the long flower stems which, at a considerable distance from the parent plant, produce new plants which strike roots. Leaves are long, narrow and grass-like. The flowers small, white stars on yellow stems.
Use: Undemanding plant for hanging bowls. Older plants with a great many flower stems and new leaf-rosettes are very decorative.
Soil: Soilless mixture. Thrives particularly well in plastic pots.
Feeding: 2 grams per litre ($\frac{3}{4}$ oz. per gallon) every week (March–October).
Water: Plenty of water from February to September, otherwise quite dry.

Light: Half-shade. During the winter as close to a window as possible.
Heat: Equally suitable for cool and warm rooms.
Air: Spray during the summertime; will stand dry room air otherwise.
Re-potting: Spring or summer. The vigorous, fleshy roots will push the plant up out of the pot, if the latter is too little and too narrow; for this reason, use large, wide pots.
Propagation: Small plants are cut from the flower stems and planted in soilless mixture mixed with sand.
Diseases: Brown leaf tips are a sign of feeding when too dry.
Variety: 'Variegatum' with a broad, white centre line along the central vein of the leaf. More decorative than the green type.

Cordyline australis

Habitat: New Zealand.
Growth: Roots white. Stem low with swollen root stock and a thick rosette 100 cm. (3 ft.) long and 20 cm. (8 in.) broad, sword-shaped, coriaceous leaves with light green central vein. The white flower tufts appear from March to May.
Use: Ornamental plant for conservatories, but too big as a room plant.
Soil: Soilless mixture or potting compost.
Feeding: 3 grams per litre (1 oz. per gallon) every 2 weeks (April–October).
Water: Summer, plentiful; winter, moderate. Will stand extended periods of drought.
Light: Well-lit, sunny situation.
Heat: May be kept out of doors during summer, on a terrace or balcony. Should be kept free from frost and well-lit during winter.
Air: Will stand dry air.
Re-potting: Every 2 years in the spring. Avoid damaging the thick, fleshy roots.
Pruning: The top can be cut off in autumn or spring, which will result in several crowns being formed.

Propagation: By seed.
Pest: Scale insect.
Other species: See below.

Cordyline indivisa

Growth: Like *Cordyline australis*, but with smaller leaves which have red central veins. Otherwise use and cultivate in the same way.

Cordyline terminalis

Growth: Leaves 50 cm. (18 in.) long and 10 cm. (4 in.) wide on stems. There are varieties with leaves in varying shades of red. Spreads branches easily.
Use and culture: As for *Cordyline australia*, but must spend the winter in a heated room at minimum 15–18°C. (60–65°F.).
Cutting: The top can be removed to induce branching.
Propagation: By cuttings of top shoots at base heat of minimum 25°C. (80°F.).

Dracaena draco

Habit: Difficult to distinguish from *Cordyline*, but it has orange-red roots and stems which are not swollen. The leaves are narrow, stiff and green.

Cordyline terminalis

Use: Young plants indoors; older ones, because of their size, best in a conservatory or greenhouse.
Soil: Light humus-rich loam or soilless mixture.
Feeding: 3 grams per litre (1 oz. per gallon) every 2 weeks (March–September).
Water: Moderate watering, but during winter should be kept quite dry.
Light: Half-shade or light.
Heat: In summer can be kept out of doors; winter, not below minimum 10°C. (50°F.).
Air: Will stand dry air.
Re-potting: From time to time during spring in pots which are not too large.
Propagation: By seed.
Pests: Scale insect, red spider mite.
Other species: See below.

Dracaena deremensis   (21)

Habitat: Tropical Africa.
Growth: Upright, with leaves 30 cm. (18 in.) long.
Use and culture: As for *Dracaena draco*, but requires higher temperatures; winter not below minimum 15°C. (60°F.).
Propagation: By cuttings.
Varieties: bausei, with a broad white central stripe along the central vein of the leaf, and *warneckii* with a number of narrow, white longitudinal stripes on the leaves.

Dracaena fragrans

Habitat: Tropical Africa.
Growth: Very broad, succulent leaves 50 cm. (20 in.) long, gathered into a rosette. Fragrant, white flowers coming from the axils.
Use and culture: As for *Dracaena draco*, but requires higher temperatures; winter, not below minimum 18°C. (65°F.). Just as undemanding with regard to light as *Aspidistra*.
Propagation: By cuttings.

Varieties: massangeana, which has leaves with a yellow central stripe, and *lindenii*, with leaves having broad, yellow strips along their edges.

Dracaena godseffiana

Habitat: Tropical Africa.
Growth: Thin stems with small, round, green leaves which have yellow dots. (The 'Florida Beauty' has particularly marked dots.) Growth is weak, which is why 3–5 plants are frequently planted together in one pot.
Use and culture: As for *Dracaena draco*, but requires higher temperatures; winter, not below minimum 18°C. (65°F.).

Dracaena marginata (22)

Habitat: Madagascar.
Growth: Narrow leaves 50 cm. (20 in.) long, with red edges.
Use and culture: As for *Dracaena draco*, but requires higher temperature; winter, not below minimum 18°C. (65°F.).

Dracaena sanderiana

Habitat: Tropical Africa.
Growth: Upright stems, with yellow-and-white-striped, lance-shaped leaves. Weak growth, which is why several plants should be planted in the same pot.
Use and culture: As for *Dracaena draco*, but requires higher temperature; winter, not below minimum 18°C. (65°F.).
[In England, 13°C. (55°F.) is quite sufficient for the last 4 species.]

Gasteria verrucosa

Habitat: South Africa.
Growth: Succulent, reminiscent of *Aloe*. The fleshy leaves grow opposite one

Gasteria verrucosa

another in two rows and are covered with dense, white spots and warts. Long flower stems with urn-shaped, orange-red flowers, spring or summer.
Use: Ideal indoor plant. Thrives in centrally heated rooms and even in full sunlight in windows facing south.
Soil: Loam mixed with sand, and possibly soilless mixture.
Feeding: 2 grams per litre ($\frac{3}{4}$ oz. per gallon) every 3 weeks (March–July).
Water: Only completely dry plants should be watered. Infrequent watering during winter. Dry plants winter best in cool rooms.
Light: Well-lit, sunny spot for growth.
Heat: Airy place during summer; winter, best at 6–8°C. (40–45°F.).
Air: Will stand dry air outstandingly well.
Re-potting: February, or after flowering has ended in June.
Propagation: By division or by cuttings of side shoots in February.
Diseases: When kept out of doors during summer in strong sunshine, leaves will turn brown. With too much moisture during winter, the plant may rot.

Haworthia margaritifera

Habitat: South Africa.
Growth: Succulent with a pretty, firm rosette, which when looked at from above is somewhat like a starfish. The leaves are dark green and thickly covered with white spots. Long, thin flower stems in spring, with a number of small bell-shaped, whitish flowers.

Use: Ideal indoor plant in full sunlight and dry air.

Soil: Loam mixed with sand or soilless mixture.

Feeding: 2 grams per litre ($\frac{1}{4}$ oz. per gallon) every 4 weeks (April–August).

Water: Summer, normal watering; winter, more sparingly, but the soil ball must never be allowed to dry out completely.

Light: Full sunlight in windows facing south.

Heat: Summer, in an airy location; winter, minimum 12° C. (54° F.).

Re-potting: February, or after flowering has ceased in June, in flat pots.

Propagation: The side shoots can be cut on re-potting and planted on their own.

NOTE: Requires higher temperature and more moisture than its close relatives, *Aloe* and *Gasteria*.

Hyacinthus orientalis (23)

Hyacinth

Habitat: Asia Minor.

Growth: Vigorous, perennial bulb with narrow leaves and flower stems bearing a large number of bell-shaped flowers.

Use: Bulb growth from the garden, which may be forced to some advantage in flower-pots or boxes with light garden soil. 'Water culture' in bulb glasses is, however, easier. The first hyacinths can be brought into bloom at Christmastime. By taking the bulbs indoors at intervals of a few weeks each time, it is possible to have flowers right through to March–April.

Soil: Normal garden soil mixed with sand, or possibly soilless mixture (which suits admirably in England), or pure water in a bulb glass.

Feeding: Unnecessary, since the plant obtains its nourishment from the bulb, but if fed the bulbs will maintain their vigour.

Water: The bulb must not be allowed to dry up once during forcing. If this happens, the roots may die or become scorched, and the plant may fail to flower.

Light: The spike must be kept dark with a black plastic sheet or a paper hood, which should remain in position until the bud emerges above the leaves. If light reaches the spike too early, the flowers may unfold down among the leaves and the stem will not elongate.

Heat: When forcing is started, as cool as possible, to correspond with natural conditions of wintering out of doors in the soil, not more than 9° C. (48° F.). When the spike is 5 cm. (2 in.) long, the bulb may be taken into room heat. When the flowers have emerged the atmosphere should be cooler once more in order to prolong the flowering period. Pre-treated ('prepared') bulbs may be forced straight away in normal room temperatures.

Air: Will stand dry room air, but the soil must be kept moist.

Suggestion for forcing in flower-pots: The bulb is placed in a pot of loam mixed with sand, half the bulb being above the surface of the soil. Water carefully, and keep completely dark in a cool cupboard or cellar, or wrapped in a black plastic bag, at minimum 9° C. (48° F.) for 8–10 weeks. When the spike is 5 cm. (2 in.) long, the pot is moved to a spot at a minimum 12° C. (54° F.), while the plastic bag is removed and replaced by a paper hood. After a further period of 2 weeks the pot is taken into a position at normal room temperature and the paper hood removed when the bud emerges. During the entire forcing period meticulous care must be taken with watering, and the soil should not be allowed to dry out completely at any time. Normally, 3 months should be allowed from potting to flowering.

Suggestion for forcing in bulb glasses: The glass is filled with water so that the lower part of the bulb just fails to touch the surface. The nose is covered with a paper hood, and the glass placed in a dark, cool spot at minimum 9° C. (48° F.) for 10 weeks. Look at the glass at least once a week, and top up the water if necessary. When the glass is filled with roots and the spike is 5 cm. (2 in.) long, place the glass in a position at minimum 12° C. (54° F.) for 2 weeks, and after this at normal room temperature. Normally, allow 3 months from putting the bulb in the glass to flowering.

Re-potting: The bulb, once forced, cannot be forced a second time, but may be put out of doors in a garden, where it will produce a fair number of flowers during subsequent years.

Propagation: By side bulbs. Must be entrusted to a bulb specialist.

Varieties: Light red: 'Pink Pearl' and 'Anne Marie'. Sky blue: 'Bismarck'. Medium blue: 'Grand Maître'. White: 'L'Innocence' and 'Queen of the Whites'. The yellow variety 'Yellow Hammer' is not suitable for forcing.

Lilium hybridum (24)

Lily

Habitat: Southern Europe, Eastern Asia and North America.

Growth: Stems 50–100 cm. (2–6 ft.) high, varying according to the different species. The leaves are narrow and shaped like arrows. The flowers are shaped like turbans, trumpets or funnels, upright in some cases and hanging in others. The colours vary from pure white through yellow to orange and red, with an infinite range of nuances. Most of them have a very strong fragrance.

Use: Prepared bulbs for *Lilium auratum* (illustrated).

Lilium longiflorum and *Lilium regale* are forced in commercial nurseries, but further forcing in outdoor culture is complicated and difficult. Pots of forced bulbs which have been purchased can, on the other hand, be used for decoration in rooms and winter gardens.

NOTE: Prepared bulbs have been sub-jected to various lengths of time at controlled temperatures, so that they will remain dormant until brought out of store and planted. In this way they can be got to flower at any season.

Soil: Deep pots with rich soil, mixed with sand, and good drainage provided by crocks, charcoal and gravel. To guard against rotting the bulb itself should be bedded on gravel, and should be covered with a layer of soil as thick as its own height.

Feeding: During the short time spent indoors, feeding is unnecessary.

Water: Plentiful from the reception of the bulb until shortly after it has finished flowering. After this, completely dry.

Light: Plenty of daylight, so that the stems remain erect.

Heat: The room temperature should not be too high.

Air: In very dry room air, gentle sprinkling is recommended during the forcing period. Otherwise, dry air.

Storage: The bulb is taken from the pot, and stored for the rest of the winter in peat litter—which should be slightly damp—or in sand in a cool cellar.

Planting out: The bulb can be planted out in the spring in a garden and it will flower here over a number of years. Forcing for a second time, however, will seldom be successful.

Species and varieties: In recent years a large number of hybrids have been produced by crossing the many known species with worthwhile characteristics, such as strong stems, attractive colours and durable flowers. The Graaf hybrids can be recommended in particular.

Sansevieria trifasciata (25)

Mother-in-law's Tongue

Habitat: Tropical Africa.

Growth: Tough, bayonet-like dark green leaves, often with attractive patterns in grey-green, silvery green and yellow. Older plants develop upright flower clusters with small greenish-white flowers. The plant often grows to a metre (3 ft.) in height with good care.

Use: Excellent indoor plant, which will stand drought and heat, and which often survives for very long periods without regular attention.

Soil: Soilless mixture or ordinary garden soil.

Feeding: 3 grams per litre (1 oz. per gallon) every week (March–September).

Water: Summer, normal; winter, very dry. Prefers dry soil ball to standing water in a base dish.

Light: Full sunlight or other very light situation. Also survives very well in darker rooms, but will not then acquire the attractive patterns on the leaves.

Heat: High room temperature does no harm. Winter, not below minimum 10° C. (50° F.).

Air: Thrives, even in the driest room air.

Re-potting: February, in pans, so that the roots cannot go too deep.

Propagation: By division of root shoots, possibly by leaf-cuttings inserted into slightly damp sand.

Diseases: None.

Varieties: 'Laurentii', with yellow leaf edges, and 'Bartels Sensation', which is only 35 cm. (15 in.) high and has white leaf edges.

Tulipa gesneriana (26)

Tulip

Habitat: Western Asia.

Growth: Fleshy, annual bulb, covered with a dry tunic. Leaves have no stems and have arched veins. The flowers have no calyces but 6 coloured perianth leaves.

Use: Among the many different types, only the earliest ones are suitable for forcing in a room, whereas none of the other garden tulips will be successful in indoor culture.

Soil: Light garden soil mixed with sand.

Feeding: Unnecessary during forcing, since the bulb contains all the nourishment necessary for flowering.

Water: Pot soil must never be allowed to dry out, before or during forcing.

Light: Up to the appearance of the buds the plant must stand in the dark. During flowering, plenty of light.

Heat: Cool 'preliminary culture' in a frame in the garden, or in a cellar or similar location. Forced best at minimum 15° C. (60° F.). When the first leaves unfold, the temperature is raised to minimum 20° C. (70° F.). In order to prolong the flowering period, the plant may again be placed in a cooler position, e.g. between double windows, when the flower has fully emerged.

Air: Moist air most suitable. Forced bulbs must never be brought into dry air or be left above a radiator.

Suggestion for forcing: Put the bulbs in pots or flat boxes and place them in a dark cellar at temperatures as low as possible. Ten weeks later root formation is in full swing and the forcing can begin in a dark room at minimum 15° C. (60° F.). When the first leaves have unfolded, put the plant in the light and raise the temperature to minimum 20° C. (70° F.), until flowering begins. The best temperature during the actual flowering period is minimum 16–18° C. (60–65° F.). Bulbs left in a cellar at 8° C. (48° F.) on 15th September can be forced at minimum 15° C. (58° F.) from 1st December and at minimum 20° C. (70° F.) from 1st January. They will then flower on about 1st February. Bulbs which have been forced once cannot be forced a second time, but after flowering has ceased they can be stored in a dry cool place and planted out in a garden in April.

Types suitable for forcing: Red: 'Brilliant Star' (particularly early and very low, so-called 'Christmas tulip'), 'Couleur cardinal', 'Prins van Oosterrijk' and 'Goya' (abundant flowering). Yellow: 'Joffre' (particularly early), 'Bellona' and 'Wilhelm Kordes' (abundant flowering). White: 'Witte Valk' and 'Schoonoord' (abundant

Veltheimia capensis

flowering). Two colours: Bi-coloured: 'Keizerskroon' (red and yellow) and 'Pink Beauty' (pink and white).
Other species: See below.

Tulipa praestans 'Fusilier' (27)

Growth: Dwarf tulip species, which is of interest in that it has many flowers on each stem. Bright red.
Use and culture: As for *Tulipa gesneriana.*

Veltheimia capensis

Habitat: South Africa.
Growth: Bulbous plant with long undulant, dark green leaves. The flower stems are 30–40 cm. (12–16 in.) high and reddish brown. The tube-like, matt, light-red flowers are gathered into a dense cluster.
Use: Durable and ideal indoor plant with long flowering period in winter. Resting period in summer.
Soil: Soilless mixture.
Feeding: 2 grams per litre ($\frac{1}{4}$ oz. per gallon) every 2 weeks (November–February).
Water: Normal, not too lavish from September to June. Should be kept com-

pletely dry during resting period from July to August.
Light: Sunny location in a window facing south. In half-shade there will be no colour on the flowers.
Heat: Winter, minimum 12–20°C. (54–68°F.); summer, normal temperature. May possibly be left to spend the summer in a warm, sunny place in the garden.
Air: Will stand dry room air.
Re-potting: The best time for re-potting in a slightly larger pot is when the leaf spike breaks through in September after the resting period has ceased. Shake off old earth, and remove dead roots. When planting, one-third of the bulb should be above the surface of the soil.
Propagation: By offshoots, which flower after developing for 3 years.

Yucca aloifolia

Habitat: Central America.
Growth: Slender stems, a metre (3 ft.) in height, with stiff, blue-green leaves provided with a prickly tip. Plants cannot flower until they are 10 years old. Large clusters with a great many bell-shaped, white, sweet-scented flowers from July to September.
Use: Space-consuming tub plant, for

Yucca aloifolia

large-scale requirements. Suitable for conservatories, verandas and patios or warm terraces during summer.

Soil: Heavy loam, with good drainage.

Feeding: 3 grams per litre (1 oz. per gallon) every week (April–September).

Water: Summer, plentiful watering, with drying out between each occasion; winter, dry.

Light: As light as possible.

Heat: Summer, normal outdoor temperature. Spring and autumn, minimum 15–20° C. (58–70° F.). Winter, only 6° C. (45° F.) in a light, unheated but frost-free room.

Air: Not sensitive to too dry air.

Re-potting: At intervals of several years.

Propagation: By cutting of root shoots, otherwise by seed.

NOTE: Avoid too much water.

Other species: See below.

Yucca recurvifolia

Growth: Type with plentiful spread of branches and yellow-striped leaves.

Use and culture: Otherwise the same as for above species.

Bromeliaceae

Aechmea fasciata (28)

Habitat: Primeval tropical forests in Central and South America.

Growth: Leaf rosette 50 cm. high and 50 cm. (20 in.) wide. Like the majority of plants of the pineapple family it is an epiphyte, which in its natural environment does not grow with its roots in the earth but on tree branches. Nourishment and water are taken through the upper sides of the leaves, and the leaf rosette stores rainwater for long periods. The roots do not develop extensively. The long, stiff leaves have toothed edges and are dark green with silvery-grey cross stripes. The small blue flowers are short-lived, but are surrounded by stiff, deep pink bracts which last for several months. The inflorescences rest upon a

Yucca recurvifolia

stiff stem, which sprouts from the middle of the leaf rosette. Only when it is 3 years old is the leaf rosette capable of flowering, and some time after flowering the rosette withers away. New inflorescences come from the side shoots at the base of the old plant.

Use: Good indoor plant, even in warm, dry rooms. After flowering has ceased, it is a decorative foliage plant.

Soil: Light soil, rich in humus (leaf mould, peat or soilless mixture).

Feeding: During the growth period in spring and summer, minute quantities of liquid fertiliser should be added to the soil at 3-weekly intervals, but *never* to the water in the leaf rosette.

Water: The soil is to be kept slightly damp, but the water itself must be administered to the leaf rosette, which should always contain moisture. Use rainwater or some other calcium-free water.

Light: As much as possible, but not in direct sunshine. Best in windows facing east, south-east, south-west and west.

Heat: Almost impossible to give it too much heat. Thrives best at a minimum 25° C. (75° F.). Minimum temperature in winter 12° C. (55° F.). At a winter temperature of below 12° C. (55° F.), growth ceases, the leaves acquire dark spots and the rosette rots.

Air: Make sure that there is plenty of fresh air in the summer. Air humidity is increased by frequent spraying.

Re-potting: Seldom necessary.
Propagation: Side shoots can be taken from older plants and put into new pots in June–July after the main rosette has ceased flowering.
Pests: Occasionally, scale insect and thrips.
NOTE: Always remember the water in the rosette.
Other species: See below.

Aechmea fulgens

Growth: Broad, semi-rigid leaf rosette. Plain, dark green leaves with reddish tinge. Blue flowers surrounded by red bracts.
Use and culture: As for *Aechmea fasciata.*

Billbergia nutans

Habitat: Mexico and South America.
Growth: Like the ordinary pineapple, a terrestial bromeliad with well-developed roots. Better suited to culture in pots than the epiphytic types. Over a period of years, produces thick tufts almost grass-like in character, 50 cm. (20 in.) high. The leaves are narrow, grooved and leathery, with sharp edges. The flowers are gathered into clusters at the tips of the nodding flower stems. The flowers are yellowy-green with blue edges, the surrounding bracts pink. The flower stalks emerge from the middle of the leaf rosette and the rosette dies after flowering has ceased. On the other hand, a number of side shoots develop, which may be left for a number of years in the same flower-pots.
Use: Easy, undemanding room plant which takes well to being left out of doors during the summer. Large plants can be cultivated in large pots or tubs in conservatories.
Soil: Loose soil, rich in humus, e.g. a mixture of leaf mould, peat and sand, possibly soilless mixture.

Feeding: Apply liquid fertiliser sparingly after flowering has ceased.
Water: Administer direct into the pot. Summer, plentiful; winter, more moderate, depending on temperature.
Light: Light spot not in direct sunlight.
Heat: Thrives best at minimum 16°C. (60°F.) the whole year round. Will, however, stand higher temperatures during winter, but not below minimum 12°C. (55°F.).
Air: Will stand dry, centrally heated air, but no draughts.
Re-potting: June–July. Water sparingly until the new roots have developed.
Propagation: By division of the larger plants on re-potting.
Pests: Scale insect.
NOTE: Along with *Sansevieria,* one of our best indoor plants in dry air.
Other species: See below.

[NOTE: In Great Britain *B. nutans* and *B. windii* are grown at somewhat lower temperatures than in Denmark, while the other species would be given higher temperatures.]

Billbergia fasciata

Growth: The tongue-shaped, bronze-green leaves, with yellowish markings and prickly edges are gathered into a 40-cm. (1-ft. 3¾-in.)-long tube. The blue flowers with bright red bracts are gathered into a nodding inflorescence.
Use and culture: As for *Billbergia nutans.*

Billbergia vittata

Growth: The tongue-shaped leaves, with white cross bands on the outer side and red spines, are gathered into a metre-long (3-ft.) tube. The leaf tips are rolled back, and the indigo blue flowers with pink bracts are gathered into a nodding inflorescence.
Use and culture: As for *Billbergia nutans.*

Cryptanthus zonatus zebrinus

Billbergia windii (29)

Growth: Vigorous *Billbergia* type. The flowers proper are long, pointed and yellowy-green. The bracts are very large and broad, and deep pink in colour.
Use and culture: As for *Billbergia nutans.*

Cryptanthus zonatus zebrinus

Habitat: Tropical forest ground plant from Brazil (individual species live as epiphytes or more often as lithophytes on rocks).
Growth: Flat leaf rosette up to 15 cm. (6 in.) across and seldom more than 3 cm. (just over an inch) high. The stiff, papery, undulant leaves are an elegant bronze-purple colour, with silvery-grey cross bands. The flowers are small and unattractive.
Use: Decorative, but not a particularly durable indoor plant. As a rule grows well only for short periods, best in a conservatory or greenhouse.
Soil: Developed best as an epiphyte, grown on a piece of bark. May also do well hanging on a piece of steel wire in a window, without any kind of root support. Treated in pots with very light soil (peat or loamless compost).
Feeding: Not necessary.
Water: Only in the leaf rosette.
Light: Requires a lot of light, but never direct sunlight.
Heat: Summer, even high temperature, approximately 25°C. (80°F.); in rest-ing period during winter, approximately 15°C. (60°F.).
Air: High degree of air humidity.
Other species: See below.

Cryptanthus bivittatus minor

Growth: Olive-green leaves with two pale, salmon-pink longitudinal stripes. In strong light or in soil which is too heavy the colour turns copper-red.
Use and culture: As for *Cryptanthus zonatus.*

Cryptanthus bromelioides tricolor

Growth: Fresh green leaves with ivory-white stripes and pink edges and base. Like a very small *Dracaena.*
Use and culture: As for *Cryptanthus zonatus.*

Guzmania monostachya

Habitat: Tropical rain forests in Central and South America.
Growth: Epiphyte with 50-cm. (20-in.)-high, funnel-shaped leaf rosette. The leaves are fully rounded at the edges and are greenish in colour. The round flower stems are covered with small red bracts with white tips. Flowers and floral bracts have black, white and red colours. The flowers last for about 14 days.

Guzmania monostachya

Use: Best in conservatories or in hothouses.
Culture: As for *Aechmea fasciata*.
Other species: See below.

Guzmania minor

Growth: 20-cm. (8-in.)-high leaf rosette. The leaves are reddish-orange. The flowers are white with red bracts. More durable than *Guzmania monostachya*. Use and culture are otherwise the same as for this type.

Neoregelia carolinae

Habitat: Tropical rain forests in Brazil.
Growth: Epiphyte with dense, flat rosette with broad leaf sheaths around the stemless, pincushion-like inflorescences. The leaves are tongue-shaped and coriaceous, with fine prickles around the edges. Both sides are green, but the innermost leaves turn blood-red when flowering takes place. The red colouring lasts for several months. The flowers are very small and reddish-violet.
Use: Best in conservatories and greenhouses.
Culture: As for *Aechmea fasciata*, but requires consistently high temperatures and high degree of air humidity all the year round.
NOTE: Limited durability. The variety *tricolor*, with leaves variegated with longitudinal yellow and cream stripes, is the form most commonly met.

Nidularium innocentii   (30)

Habitat: Brazil. The Latin name, which means 'little bird's nest', refers to the inflorescences, which are right in the middle of the leaf rosettes.
Growth: As for *Neoregelia carolinae*, from which it may be difficult to distinguish. The leaves are broadest at the bottom and have toothed edges; their upper side is dark green, the underside

blackish-green. The central leaves remain bright copper red during the whole of the flowering period. The inconspicuous white flowers are hidden in the 'bird's nest'.
Use: Best in a hothouse.
Culture: As for *Aechmea fasciata*, but requires constant high temperature, ample degree of air humidity and shade.
NOTE: Limited durability indoors.
Other species: See below.

Nidularium fulgens

Growth: Leaves are pale green with dark green spots and serrated edges. The central leaves are scarlet, the flowers violet with white tubes.
Use and culture: As for *Nidularium innocentii*.

Tillandsia cyanea   (31)

Habitat: Ecuador.
Growth: Elegant leaf rosette, which readily develops side shoots. The leaves are dark green, narrow and sharp-edged. The 20-cm. (8-in.)-high flower stem ends at the top in a flat diamond-shaped, light red spike, and the large individual flowers emerge between the bracts of this, one at a time. They are an intense blue in colour, and although each is short-lived the complete flowering extends over a long period.
Use: Good and durable indoor plant.
Culture: As for *Aechmea fasciata*.
Other species: See below.

Tillandsia lindenii

Growth: Larger than *Tillandsia cyanea*, up to 50 cm. (20 in.) in height. Use and culture otherwise as for this species.

Vriesia hieroglyphica

Habitat: Tropical rain forests in Central and South America.
Growth: Leaf rosette up to 50 cm.

Vriesia hieroglyphica

(20 in.) in height, and of equal width; each leaf 6–8 cm. (2–3 in.) broad, with a sharp tip. The colour is grey-green, with brownish, uneven transverse stripes which are somewhat reminiscent of handwritten characters, hence the name. Cultivated for the sake of the attractive leaves. The flowers are spread out on a 50-cm. (20-in.)-high stem, and the plant can only flower after 4 years' growth.

Use: Durable and well suited to cultivation in a room or a conservatory.

Culture: As for *Aechmea fasciata*. Must be protected, especially against direct sunlight. Only use water which is calcium-free, which should be poured directly into the leaf rosette. Re-potting unnecessary.

Diseases: Yellow leaves are a sign of too much sunlight.

Other species: See below.

Vriesia splendens (32)

Growth: Leaves 4–6 cm. (1½–2½ in.) broad, vivid green in colour, with brown cross stripes. A broad, thick, sword-shaped spike protrudes from the leaf rosette. The flowers are yellow and short-lived, while the fiery red bracts remain for a long time. May flower at any time.

Use and culture: As for *Vriesia hieroglyphica*, but give more light.

Amaryllidaceae

Agave americana (33)

Century Plant

Habitat: Mexico and Central America.

Growth: Rigid, fleshy leaves, gathered into a decorative rosette. The leaf edges are prickly and the leaf tip has a very sharp spine which may be a danger to anyone in the plant's immediate vicinity. The leaves are blue-green, often with yellow longitudinal stripes or edges. Only the older plants flower, with a 2–5-m. (6½–16-ft.)-high flower stem, after which the plant dies.

Use: Very large tub plant for conservatories, suitable for patios and terraces during the summer. The leaf tips are provided with cork stops during transport, to avoid accidents. Should not be kept in homes where there are small children.

Soil: Soilless mixture.

Feeding: 3 grams per litre (1 oz. per gallon) every 2 weeks (March–September).

Water: Plenty during the summer, dry in winter.

Light: Light, sunny growth spot, particularly in winter.

Heat: Summer, best out of doors; winter, minimum 4–8° C. (40–45° F.). Will not stand frost.

Air: Likes dry air.

Re-potting: Every 3 years in February.

Propagation: By cutting the small rosettes on the runners.

Diseases: Brown spots on leaves from too much warmth, darkness or humidity during winter.

Variant: 'Variegata', with yellow stripes along the edges of the leaves.

NOTE: Take care with the spiny leaf tips.

Other species: See below.

Agave filifera

Growth: No prickly edges, but with a row of bristles along the edges of the leaves.
Use and culture: As for *Agave americana*.

Clivia miniata (34)

Kaffir Lily

Habitat: South Africa.
Growth: Fleshy roots. Thick leaf sheaths with dark green leaves, which branch out alternately on both sides. The 50-cm. (20-in.)-high, flat flower stems bear 10–20 orange-red-coloured flowers in the spring, and occasionally also in the autumn.
Use: Undemanding, perennial indoor plant, which must always be kept in the same place and position. Not even the pot should be turned.
Soil: Soilless mixture, or heavy, somewhat clayey garden soil. pH 7.
Feeding: 3 grams per litre (1 oz. per gallon) every week (March–August).
Water: Will not stand constant moisture. During the growth period from February to August, the pot must be allowed to dry out between each thorough watering. During the resting period from September to January, the plant must be allowed to remain completely dry.
Light: Best in a light window with slight shade.
Heat: Normal room temperature, not below minimum 15° C. (60° F.). When temperatures are too low during the development of flowers, the flower stems will not have the desired length, and the flowers will remain down in between the leaves. In the resting period in autumn and winter, best at minimum 12° C. (55° F.).
Air: Will stand dry room air, but likes syringing during growth period *after* flowering has ceased.
Re-potting: After flowering has ceased,

Eucharis grandiflora

in spacious pots. Careful watering after re-potting, so that the fleshy roots do not rot.
Cutting: The flower stems are cut out in the normal way after flowering has ceased.
Propagation: By division after flowering has ceased. Second-year plants are generally capable of flowering.
NOTE: Failure to flower may be due to the fact that the resting period has not been properly provided for.

Eucharis grandiflora

Habitat: South America.
Growth: The leaves are arum-like. The 50-cm. (20-in.)-high, upright flower stems are without leaves. The lily-like, pure white, delicately fragrant flowers have a perianth with jagged edges and green stripes. Continuously flowering so long as growth is not retarded.
Use: Somewhat difficult indoor plant, which requires constant humidity and a temperature of minimum 20° C. (70° F.) all the year round.
Soil: Deep pots with at least 20 cm. (8 in.) of soil, consisting of strong earth mould, with leaf mould and sand mixed in.
Feeding: 2 grams per litre ($\frac{3}{4}$ oz. per

gallon) every week (March–October). Incorporate plenty of bonemeal in the potting compost.

Water: Grows in nature in river deltas, which is why it needs constant watering and must never dry out.

Light: Best in a light window, but never ·in direct sunlight.

Heat: Very demanding with regard to heat, not below minimum 20° C. (70° F.).

Air: Humid air with frequent syringing.

Re-potting: Every 2 years. The bulb tips must be flush with the surface of the soil.

Propagation: By side bulbs with at least one leaf.

NOTE: Flowers attractive, and durable when out.

Haemanthus albiflos

Habitat: South Africa.

Growth: Bulbous plant, with a few evergreen, downy leaves. Flowers are white with bunches of yellow stamens and gathered into an inflorescence like a shaving brush. Flowers in the spring.

Use: Durable and rewarding indoor plant, even in centrally heated rooms.

Soil: Soilless mixture.

Feeding: 2 grams of fertiliser per litre ($\frac{1}{2}$ oz. per gallon) of water every 2 weeks (May–July). Plants which receive too much nourishment have difficulty in getting through the winter.

Water: Normal watering in summer; from August to the end of January, very dry. Will prefer being dried out completely to being overwatered.

Light: Full sunlight.

Heat: Normal room temperature; in winter best at minimum 12–16° C. (55–60° F.).

Air: Dry air.

Re-potting: Every 2 years. Only half of the bulb must be covered with soil.

Propagation: By division.

Other species: See below.

Haemanthus katherinae

Growth: Vigorous. The undulant green leaves wither in the autumn. The large inflorescence has deep red flowers, with blood-red stamens and pistils. The flowering season is during the height of the summer. The name 'Blood-flower' relates to the red sap which appears when the leaves or stems are lacerated.

Use and culture: As for *Haemanthus albiflos*, but requires higher temperature and higher degree of air humidity.

Haemanthus puniccus   (35)

Growth: Shorter stems and smaller flowers than the other *Haemanthus* species. The flowers are bright red.

Use and culture: As for *Haemanthus albiflos*, but requires higher degree of air humidity.

Hippeastrum hortorum   (36)
Amaryllis

Habitat: South America.

Growth: Vigorous bulb with fleshy roots. The leaves are long and ribbon-like. One or two strong flower stems, each with 4–6 trumpet-shaped flowers in white, pale red or dark red.

Use: Easy forcing plant for flowering at Christmas or after.

Soil: Soilless mixture, with good drainage. Only half of the bulb must be covered with soil.

Feeding: 5 grams of fertiliser per litre ($1\frac{1}{2}$ oz. per gallon) of water every 2 weeks from the end of flowering to the beginning of the resting period in September–October. No feeding during the flowering season.

Water: Dry during the resting period and until the flower shoot has emerged. After that, plentiful watering during the flowering and growing season in spring and summer.

Light: Light and sunny situation from

the end of flowering until October. Remember to keep the flower shoot in shade during its development, so as to assist the lengthening of the stem.

Heat: During forcing, minimum 20–25° C. (70–80° F.). Afterwards, cooler. In summer, out of doors on a balcony or in a garden.

Air: Spray during the development of leaves and flowers.

Re-potting: Every 3 or 4 years in larger pots. Only half of the bulbs flower when forced a second time, therefore attempts at this are usually disappointing.

Propagation: By seed or side bulbs.

Suggestion for forcing: Having bought the bulbs, place them in lukewarm water for 24 hours. Then plant them in soilless mixture in plastic pots with at least 2 cm. (¾ in.) drainage at the bottom. The soil should only cover half the bulb, and should be loose underneath and around it. The bulb should then be covered with a paper hood, and placed in direct heat, possibly near a radiator. Give just enough water to ensure that the soil does not dry out completely. Water more generously when the spike is 10 cm. (4 in.) long, and remove the paper hood. Care with watering and feeding after flowering is important if there is to be the possibility of forcing and flowering again the following year. The resting period, October–December, must not be neglected; during this time the leaves die and the old roots dry up, and the plant must be kept cool, protected from frost and absolutely dry.

NOTE: You can only depend on flowering if you force new bulbs each year. A better result is obtained with *Vallota speciosa*, which see.

Hymenocallis speciosa

Habitat: West Indies.

Growth: Vigorous bulb plant with broad, ribbon-like leaves. The white flowers, which have a vanilla fragrance, are gathered 10–12 together into an

Hymenocallis speciosa

umbel, the outer ones opening out first. Flowering may take place at any time during the year, though normally in the autumn.

Use: Hothouse plant, which requires a high soil and air temperature the whole year round. No real resting period. Well suited for warm conservatory or greenhouse.

Soil: Soilless mixture (in large pots).

Feeding: 3 grams of fertiliser per litre of water (1 oz. per gallon) each week during the summer.

Water: Summer, frequent watering. During the winter use only water with the chill taken off it. The soil must not be cooled by cold water.

Light: Plenty, but no direct sunlight.

Heat: Best at minimum 20° C. (70° F.) the whole year round.

Air: Summer, humid air; winter, drier.

Re-potting: After flowering has ceased. Avoid lacerating or drying out the roots.

Propagation: By side bulbs.

Other species: See below.

Hymenocallis macrostephana

Habitat: Bolivia.

Growth: Flowers in the summer.

Use and culture: As for *Hymenocallis speciosa*, but does not require quite such high temperatures. Resting period from September to March, during which the bulb should be kept dry and cool at a minimum 10° C. (50° F.).

Narcissus pseudonarcissus (37)

Daffodil

Habitat: Western Europe.

Growth: Vigorous, perennial bulb with narrow linear leaves. Only one flower on each stem. The flower has a protruding, collar-like perianth and a trumpet-shaped corona.

Use: As easy to force as *Hyacinthus orientalis*, but best at relatively low temperature.

Soil: Ordinary garden soil mixed with sand.

Feeding: Unnecessary before and during forcing, since the bulb contains the nutrients necessary for flowering.

Water: The soil must never dry out; generous watering is thus required.

Light: The spike must be protected from the daylight by a paper hood, as for hyacinth forcing.

Heat: During the development of roots, minimum 5° C. (40° F.), afterwards minimum 10° C. (50° F.). When the flower buds appear, at minimum 15° C. (60° F.), and when they open out, ordinary room temperature.

Air: Thrives in dry centrally heated air, but likes syringing during forcing.

Re-potting: The bulbs cannot be forced a second time, but can be used in the garden. The forced bulbs must be put out of doors as soon as they can be got into the soil.

Propagation: By side bulbs.

Suggestion for forcing in pots: Preference should be given to large 'double-nosed' bulbs, since each 'nose' produces one flower. They are placed in 5-in. pots in August–September, and kept in a cool cellar at a minimum 5° C. (40° F.) for 6 weeks; afterwards at a minimum 10° C. (50° F.) for 4 weeks; for a time at a minimum 15° C. (60° F.), until the flower stems grow longer; finally, at normal room temperature. In order to obtain sufficiently long stems, the paper hood is not removed until the bud is beginning to emerge. The bulbs must be inspected regularly to ensure that the soil never dries out. After flowering, the bulbs are placed in a light, cool place, but are kept regularly watered, until they can be planted out in the garden in April.

Forcing in a bulb jar: Like hyacinths, the bulbs can also be forced in a bulb jar, but unlike them, they must not come into contact with the water. The heavy top part must be supported so that it does not overturn.

Forcing in artificial light: Narcissus bulbs may be forced with 12 hours' daylight. The plant's natural flowering takes place at the spring equinox, when it is affected by the regular alternation between 12 hours of daylight and 12 hours of darkness. The bulbs should be planted as usual in pots or boxes and kept in earth pits or cellars at low temperatures. When the spikes are 5 cm. (2 in.) long late in November the bulbs are placed in a cellar, where, with the aid of lamp bulbs or fluorescent tubes, they are given 12 hours' light alternated with 12 hours' darkness. The lamps should give off 1,000 watts per square yard of floor area, and be suspended at 100 cm. (3 ft.) above the plants. Air temperature should be a minimum 18° C. (65° F.). When the buds begin to colour, the bulbs are taken into the house.

Types suitable for forcing: 'Golden Harvest' and 'King Alfred'.

Other species: See below.

Narcissus tazetta totus albus

Paper-white Narcissus

Growth: A large number of small, star-shaped flowers on each stem. Delicate fragrance.

Narcissus totus albus

Forcing: The bulbs are planted in dishes with gravel or pebbles, at normal room temperatures for 7 weeks without pre-culture, in a cool, dark atmosphere. There should be standing water in the dish the whole time, up to the middle of the bulb. The bulbs are discarded after flowering once, and cannot be used in the garden since they are not sufficiently hardy for our climate.

Narcissus poetaz (38)

Growth: Several small, cup-shaped flowers with a little, flat corona on each stem. Delicate fragrance.

Varieties suitable for forcing: Abundant flowering: 'Cheerfulness' (cream coloured). Single flowers: 'Scarlet Gem' (pale yellow and orange-yellow) and 'Geranium' (white and orange-yellow). These varieties can be forced as indicated for *Narcissus pseudonarcissus.* 'Cragford' (white and orange) may be forced in dishes with pebbles and water, like *Narcissus totus albus.*

Sprekelia formosissima (39)

Jacobean Lily

Habitat: Mexico.

Growth: Dark bulbs, narrow ribbon-like leaves and an unusual, cross-shaped, velvet-red flower, the shape of which is reminiscent of the cross of the Spanish Crusaders' patron saint, Saint James of Calatrava.

Use: Summer-flowering bulb plant for rooms, winter gardens or warm sunny spots out of doors. Should be planted in early spring, flowers in May–June, and is taken up in the autumn for warm and dry wintering.

Soil: Soilless mixture.

Feeding: 3 grams of fertiliser per litre (1 oz. per gallon) of water every week, May–July.

Water: After planting, water carefully, but more copiously when the leaves appear. Watering should be stopped when the leaves wither in August, and the plant should be kept completely dry for the rest of the year.

Light: Sunlight.

Heat: Summer, normal temperature; winter, minimum 12° C. (55° F.). If kept too cool during the winter, it will not flower the following summer.

Air: Normal, dry indoor air.

Re-potting: January–February, before growth gets under way.

Propagation: By side bulbs. Seedlings flower when 4 years old.

Vallota speciosa (40)

Scarborough Lily

Habitat: South Africa.

Growth: Reminiscent of *Amaryllis*, but less vigorous and flowers in August–September. The bulb is brown, the leaves and stems 30 cm. (12 in.) high, the flowers bright red.

Use: Very attractive and good, late-summer flowering indoor plant. Easily flowers a second time. Resents root disturbances and thrives in the same pot for many years.

Soil: Soilless mixture.

Feeding: 3 grams of fertiliser per litre (1 oz. per gallon) of water every 2 weeks (March–August).

Water: Normal watering during the whole of the growth period until flowering. Afterwards, only small amounts, and completely dry in winter. Very young plants should, however, have slightly moist soil balls even in winter.

Light: Likes full sunlight.

Heat: Normal room temperature. Older, flowering plants should spend the winter at minimum 12°C. (55°F.), young plants at minimum 15–20°C. (60–70°F.) so that they can continue their growth without a period of rest.

Air: Will stand dry room air.

Re-potting: Early spring in pots which are not too large. The fleshy roots must be handled with care, so that they do not snap or become damaged.

Propagation: By side bulbs, which will flower after 3 years' development.

NOTE: An easy, summer-flowering bulb plant which may be recommended.

Zephyranthes grandiflora

Habitat: Central America.

Growth: Small, short-necked, oval bulb with 20-cm. (8-in.) linear leaves. The stems bear one erect, funnel-shaped flower, which is luminous pink in colour.

Use: Attractive spring- and summer-flowering bulb plant for rooms and con-servatories. When not in flower, the plant has no attraction.

Soil: Soilless mixture.

Feeding: 2 grams of fertiliser per litre ($\frac{3}{4}$ oz. per gallon) of water every 2 weeks in summer.

Water: Summer, plentiful; winter, more sparingly, but without allowing the soil to dry out completely.

Light: Sunny spot.

Heat: Normal room temperature; winter, now below minimum 10°C. (50°F.). Will not stand frost at all.

Air: Will stand dry room air.

Re-potting: Spring, before growth begins.

Propagation: Develops a number of side bulbs.

Orchidaceae

Orchids

Habitat: The orchid family covers a large number of genera, from a wide variety of climatic conditions, with varying temperature, air humidity and soil requirements.

Growth: Many orchids are epiphytes. When growing wild, their roots suck in nourishment from rotten plant fragments and moss on tree bark. Others grow with their roots directly in the earth, often in symbiosis with certain types of fungus.

Use: Most orchids are only suitable for cultivation in specially arranged greenhouses or flower windows. Few can be used for normal indoor culture. A very few are fragrant. Orchids have a number of cultural requirements in common, which are described immediately below, while the special requirements are indicated for the individual types.

Soil: Orchid soil is a mixture consisting of fern fibres (from Osmunda- or tree-ferns), peat, sphagnum moss, beech leaves and bark. The nutrients in this light soil are converted more rapidly

Zephyranthes grandiflora

than those in ordinary soil, which is why orchids must be frequently re-potted, and the intervals between re-potting depend on the consistency of the soil mixture. In the U.S.A. the epiphytic species are more commonly potted in chunks of fir bark, sold under various trade names.

Other common culture requirements: Rainwater or some other soft water must be used for watering. Nourishment requirements are more modest than for other indoor plants (half quantities). Temperature requirements vary for the different kinds and must be adhered to rigidly. If the resting period is not observed, flowering will fail.

Genera and species: See below.

Cattleya labiata (41)

Cattleya

Habitat: Central and South America.

Growth: Creeping rhizome with thick pseudo-bulbs, each with one or two coriaceous, evergreen leaves. The inflorescence emerges from the latest developed pseudo-bulb and has one or more flowers. Every flower has 3 sepals and 3 petals, of which one—the lip—is the largest and has the deepest colour. Many colours are represented: white, yellow, pink, mauve, violet and red. Flowering begins a few months after the bulb has reached full growth; after flowering, there is a resting period of 4 weeks, during which no water should be given.

Use: Hybrids are more suitable for indoor culture.

Soil: Compost, consisting of fern fibre, sphagnum and beech leaves.

Feeding: 1 gram of fertiliser per litre ($\frac{1}{4}$ oz. per gallon) of water every 2 weeks during the growth period. (Most orchid growers never use fertiliser except as a foliar feed.)

Water: Water generously during the summer, while the soil should be

Coelogyne cristata

allowed to dry out between each watering during the winter. No water during the resting period.

Light: Requires as much light as possible. Flower-pots or plant-boxes must, however, be protected against direct sunlight.

Heat: Minimum 20° C. (70° F.) during the day, somewhat cooler at night. Minimum temperature in winter 14° C. (57° F.).

Air: Will stand dry room air very well. Frequent syringing during hot weather.

Re-potting: After flowering, when the compost has decayed and is loose. Take care that the plant is bedded in firmly.

Propagation: By division. With every pseudo-bulb which is separated from the parent plant, a latent bud should develop.

NOTE: Concerning culture requirements in general, see *Orchids.*

Coelogyne cristata

Habitat: Ceylon, East Indies and Samoa.

Growth: Fleshy, slightly wrinkled pseudo-bulbs, pointed leaves and hanging inflorescences with white, yellow-edged flowers, October–November.

Use: Easy indoor orchid, which must be kept during the summer in a slightly shaded place in the garden, and possibly suspended in the crown of a tree.

Soil: Cultivated in a box or pot with compost, consisting of sphagnum, shredded bark and beech leaves.

Feeding: 1 gram of fertiliser per litre ($\frac{1}{4}$ oz. per gallon) of water every 3 weeks during the growth period.

Water: Water generously in summer; after flowering, relatively dry.

Light: Slight shade in a window facing east, west or north.

Heat: Minimum 15–20° C. (60–70° F.).

Air: Likes humid air, best in living-rooms or kitchens with a high degree of air humidity. Frequent sprinkling, especially during hot weather.

Re-potting: As for *Cattleya labiata.*

Culture requirements in general, see *Orchids.*

Cymbidium pumilum (42)

Habitat: China and Japan.

Growth: Epiphyte, with a short rhizome which has a large number of small, long-lasting white, yellow and brown flowers in the winter.

Special culture requirements: Good indoor orchid under cool conditions—a winter temperature of 10° C. (50° F.) and summer temperature not exceeding 21° C. (70° F.). Cultivated in orchid soil in plastic pots with good drainage. Large amounts of light and water during the growth period. A resting period of 4 weeks in the autumn is necessary for flowering. Concerning culture requirements in general, see *Orchids.*

NOTE: A very tricky indoor plant for amateurs.

Paphiopedilum (Cypripedium) hybridum (43)

Slipper Orchid

Habitat: Tropical Asia.

Growth: Winter-flowering terrestial orchid without pseudo-bulbs. Decorative leaves, often with attractive markings in dark green and brown. The flowers, which are borne singly on rigid stems and are very durable, have a waxy appearance with dark, shoe-shaped lips and lighter perianths with attractive patterns in white, yellow, green and brown. Innumerable varieties.

Use: Easy indoor orchid for flower pots, preferably plastic pots with good drainage. The green-leafed varieties are best in cool locations. Those with mottled leaves do well in normal room temperatures. A 5-week resting period, September–October, is necessary for flowering in January–February.

Soil: Sphagnum, with shredded bark and beech leaves added.

Feeding: 1 gram of fertiliser per litre ($\frac{1}{4}$ oz. per gallon) of water every 2 weeks during the growth period.

Water: Ordinary tap water (not rainwater). Give even watering the whole year round and never allow to become bone-dry. Should only be dry during resting period and immediately after re-potting.

Light: Slight shade.

Heat: Normal room temperature, but only minimum 10–12° C. (50–55° F.) during resting period.

Air: Spray during hot periods.

Re-potting: After flowering has ceased, late winter. Firm potting. No water for 14 days afterwards.

NOTE: If the resting period is not observed, flowering will fail, which applies to all the *Paphiopedilum* types.

Other species: See below.

Dendrobium nobile

Habitat: Southern Asia and Australia.

Growth: Epiphyte with long, thin pseudobulbs, each with 2–3 flowers in pink, violet and white in early spring. The roots spread themselves out on the surface of the soil.

Use: Rewarding indoor plant which flowers annually.

Soil: Cultivated in a very small pot with just a little orchid soil. The bottom two-thirds of the pot are filled with broken

Dendrobium nobile

crocks for drainage, so as to avoid constant moisture. An orchid basket is also suitable for cultivation.

Feeding: 1 gram fertiliser per litre of water ($\frac{1}{4}$ oz. per gallon) every 3 weeks during the growth period.

Water: Frequent watering, since the compost quickly dries out with the efficient drainage arrangement used. New shoots will rot with excessive moisture. When the bulbs have developed sufficiently the plant must be kept completely dry during the winter, until the flower buds are just developing.

Light: Plenty of light.

Heat: Very warm during the summer, winter cool (minimum 6–15° C. or 45–60° F.). A high winter temperature coupled with dampness produces a number of small plants instead of flower buds.

Air: Frequent sprinkling in hot weather.

Re-potting: After flowering has ceased.

Concerning culture requirements in general, see *Orchids*.

Other species: See below.

Dendrobium phalaenopsis

Growth: Large stems with 10–20 long-lasting flowers in autumn and winter. Pink, dark purple and white varieties.

Culture requirements: As for *Dendrobium nobile,* but to be cultivated in warmth the whole year round.

NOTE: Very difficult plant for amateurs.

Epidendrum vitellinum

Habitat: Mountainous regions in Mexico.

Growth: Compact plant with short, thick pseudo-bulbs, having durable, orange-red flowers measuring 5 cm. (nearly 2 in.) in great profusion on 20-cm. (8-in.)-high stems.

Special culture requirements: Fares best at steady, cool room temperatures and in large amounts of light. No definite resting period. Concerning cultural requirements in general, see *Orchids*.

Odontoglossum grande   (44)

Habitat: Cool mountainous regions in Tropical America.

Growth: Winter-flowering plant with 3–5 very large, yellow flowers with brown blotches and stripes.

Special culture requirements: Easy indoor orchid under cool conditions (minimum 15° C. or 60° F.) and heavy shade, e.g. in a light window facing north. Can be left to spend the summer

Epidendrum vitellinum

in a garden. Concerning culture requirements in general, see *Orchids*.
Other species: See below.

Odontoglossum pulchellum

Growth: Shining pure white flowers with yellow spots on the lips. It is very fragrant.
Culture: As for *Odontoglossum grande*.

Oncidium ornithorhynchum (45)

Habitat: Tropical America.
Growth: Epiphyte with thick pseudobulbs and flower stems 30 cm. (12 in.) long, bearing a very large number of small mauve flowers in autumn and winter. Delicate fragrance.
Special culture requirements: Cultivated on a block of bark or in a basket, so as to avoid constant dampness at the roots. Slightly shaded situation in a room which is not too warm (minimum 15° C. or 60° F.). Concerning culture requirements in general, see *Orchids*.

Paphiopedilum callosum

Growth: Marbled leaves and white-green flowers with brownish-violet stripes.
Use and culture: As for *Paphiopedilum hybridum*, but best at minimum 18° C. (65° F.).

Paphiopedilum insigne

Growth: Green leaves. Flowers white or pale green with brown markings.
Use and culture: As for *Paphiopedilum hybridum*, but requires somewhat lower temperature (minimum 14° C. or 55° F.).

Paphiopedilum villosum

Growth: Light brown flowers. Vigorous growth.

Calathea insignis

Use and culture: As for *Paphiopedilum hybridum*, but best at minimum 16° C. (60° F.).

Marantaceae

Calathea insignis

Habitat: Damp forests in Tropical America.
Growth: Foliage plant with light green leaves bearing attractive, leaf-shaped markings in dark green.
Use: Heat demanding plant. Best in warm conservatories, or as a short-lived ornamental plant in warm rooms.
Soil: Soilless mixture with good drainage.
Feeding: 3 grams of fertiliser per litre (1 oz. per gallon) of water every 2 weeks (March–August).
Water: Never allow to dry out completely, but must not be too damp, especially in the winter-time.
Light: Full or half-shade.
Heat: Best at minimum 22–25° C. (70–80° F.), never below 15° C. (60° F.).
Air: High degree of air humidity, frequent spraying the whole year round.
Re-potting: Spring, in pots which are not too large.
Propagation: By division.
Pests: Red spider mites.

Maranta leuconeura kerchoveana (46)

Prayer Plant

Habitat: Tropical America.

Growth: 20-cm. (8-in.)-high foliage plant, with green, oval leaves which have pairs of dark green spots on both sides of the midrib. On young leaves the markings are olive-green or brown. The leaf veins stand out and are silvery-grey, like fishbones. During the evening and night, the leaves turn themselves in pairs into a vertical sleeping position.

Use: Ornamental foliage plant in slightly shaded flower windows or winter gardens.

Soil: Soilless mixture.

Feeding: 1 gram of fertiliser per litre ($\frac{1}{4}$ oz. per gallon) of water every 2 weeks (April–August).

Water: Never allow to dry out completely, as this will cause brown edges on the leaves.

Light: Half-shade, never direct sunlight.

Heat: Requires a lot of heat; winter, not below minimum 18°C. (65°F.).

Air: Will not stand draughts. Best in humid air. Sprinkling with lime-free water during the summer.

Re-potting: February, in pans with ample drainage.

Propagation: By division.

Pests: Slugs and snails, wood lice.

Moraceae

Ficus benjamina (47)

Habitat: The Tropics.

Growth: Loose, pendulous growth, like a birch tree. Small, pointed dark green leaves.

Use: Elegant indoor plant, which, however, under good conditions quickly grows too large for an ordinary windowsill. Well suited for conservatories or as an ornamental plant for larger rooms.

Soil: Soilless mixture (very large pots).

Feeding: 3 grams of fertiliser per litre (1 oz. per gallon) of water every 2 weeks (February–September). Never feed during winter.

Water: Water generously during the summer; avoid drying out completely. The pot should be evenly damp during the winter.

Light: Semi-shaded or light situation. In heavy shade the leaves are gradually shed.

Heat: Normal room temperature; winter, best at minimum 16–20°C. (60–70°F.).

Air: Dry room air.

Re-potting: Early spring.

Propagation: By cuttings, with high bottom heat.

Pests: Red spider mites.

Other species: See below.

Ficus carica (48)

Fig

Habitat: Mediterranean countries and the Orient.

Growth: Deciduous tree with attractive, pale grey bark, sharply lobed leaves and green or violet pleasant-tasting fruits.

Use: May be cultivated in cool conservatories, cold greenhouses or out of doors in protected locations on south walls, possibly as a tub plant on a terrace, wintering in a light frost-free room. Small plants are decorative on windowsills. Seldom bears fruit indoors.

Soil: Standard potting mixture or garden soil with peat and sand added.

Feeding: 6 grams of fertiliser per litre (2 oz. per gallon) of water every 2 weeks during the growth period.

Water: Water generously in the spring and early summer, after which keep dry, and in winter completely dry.

Light: As light as possible.

Heat: Summer, normal temperature; winter, minimum 5°C. (40°F.).

Air: Spraying during growth period.

Re-potting: When the roots fill the pot or tub.

Ficus diversifolia

Cutting: Plants which are too big can be cut back in the late autumn or in winter.
Propagation: By seed (or by rooting suckers).

Ficus diversifolia

Mistletoe Fig

Habitat: Tropical rain forests in Java.
Growth: Bush-like, with oval leaves which have small black dots on their undersides. The tiny, berry-like, red or yellow fruits are found in great profusion.
Use: Decorative 'fruit plant' in semi-shaded windows.
Culture: As for *Ficus benjamina.*

Ficus elastica   (49)

India Rubber Plant

Habitat: Tropical rain forests in Eastern Asia.
Growth: Vigorous, erect plant, with shiny, coriaceous, dark green leaves. Removing the growing point will cause branching.

Use: Good indoor plant, even in shady rooms. Best in the same location the whole year round.
Culture: As for *Ficus benjamina.* Best winter temperature, however, minimum 15°C. (60°F.).
Pests: Red spider mites in too harsh sunlight, scale insects, mealy bug.
Diseases: The bottom leaves are shed when the plant lacks nourishment. If the winter conditions are too damp the plant is easily destroyed. With too much heat the leaves hang down limply.
Varieties: decora, which has broad, oval leaves and is not very demanding; *schyveriana*, with broad, greenish-yellow marbled leaves, and 'Variegata' with narrow, white or yellow multi-coloured leaves.
NOTE: Clean dusty leaves with soft soapy water (not synthetic detergent), and rinse with plain water, preferably rainwater.

Ficus lyrata

Fiddle-leaf Fig

Habitat: West Africa.
Growth: Large, violin-shaped, shiny leaves.

Ficus lyrata

Ficus radicans

Use: Not so durable in a room, best in a conservatory or a hall.
Culture: As for *Ficus benjamina*. Will not stand draughts or temperatures which are too low.

Ficus pumila   (50)

Creeping Fig

Habitat: China, Japan and Australia.
Growth: Climbing plant with small, dense, oval leaves. Without a base or support for the suction roots the plant will take on a hanging growth.
Use: Suitable as a hanging-bowl plant or as creeping ground covering in flower windows or conservatories.
Culture: As for *Ficus benjamina*, but will thrive under much cooler conditions and requires constant shade.
Variant: minima, with leaves which are hardly 1 cm. ($\frac{2}{5}$ in.) long.

Ficus radicans

Growth: More vigorous than *Ficus pumila* with large, pointed leaves and the same creeping growth. Runners up to 5 metres (15 ft.) long under good conditions in a conservatory or hothouse. Used and cultivated otherwise as the species described above.

Ficus religiosa

'Peepul'

Habitat: East Indies and Ceylon. The Buddhists' holy tree, under which—according to tradition—Buddha saw his visions. Offshoots are planted in temples all over the East.
Growth: A deciduous tree having more than one trunk with elegant poplar-like leaves with extended tips.
Use: Suitable for conservatories and greenhouses.
Culture: As for *Ficus benjamina*.

Urticaceae

Helxine soleirolii

'Mind your own business'
Known exclusively in U.S.A. as **'Baby's Tears'**

Habitat: Corsica.
Growth: Low, creeping, succulent-green plant with small, rounded leaves. Quickly covers the pot and hangs down over the sides.
Use: Hanging-bowl plant. Apart from this, it is suitable as a ground covering

Ficus religiosa

for conservatories, flower windows or vivaria.

Soil: Soilless mixture.

Feeding: 2 grams of fertiliser per litre ($\frac{1}{2}$ oz. per gallon) of water every 2 weeks, as far as possible without moistening the leaves with the water, which may scorch the foliage.

Water: Heavy consumption of water in summer; less in autumn and winter. Should never be allowed to dry out completely. Water may be put into a base dish and the water which has not been absorbed emptied after half an hour.

Light: Thrives in both light and shade. When kept warm during the winter should have as well-lit a location as possible so as to avoid long, etiolated shoots.

Heat: Normal room temperature.

Air: Will stand dry room air, but it is as well to sprinkle during the hot season.

Re-potting: Early spring.

Propagation: By division in the spring in pots which are not too large.

Pests: Snails and slugs.

Helxine soleirolii

Pilea nummulariifolia

Pilea nummulariifolia

Gunpowder plant

Habitat: West Indies.

Growth: Creeping plant with scabrous, yellowy-green leaves and small, pale green flowers, the anthers of which, on ripening, spring into an upright position and eject a cloud of dust into the air, whence the common name.

Use: Hanging-bowl plant for a shaded room.

Soil: Standard potting mixture.

Feeding: 3 grams of fertiliser per litre (1 oz. per gallon) of water every week (March–September).

Water: Summer, normal watering; winter, moderate.

Light: Full or half shade.

Heat: Room temperature should not be too high; winter, best at minimum 15° C. (60° F.).

Air: Air should for preference be humid in spring, otherwise normal room air.

Re-potting: February.

Propagation: By cuttings in the spring.

Pests: Slugs and snails.

Other species: See below.

189

Pilea cadierei

Pilea cadierei

Aluminium plant

Habitat: Vietnam.
Growth: 30-cm. (12-in.)-high foliage plant. The large, dark green leaves have 4 rows of aluminium-coloured spots and, between these, 3 distinct longitudinal stripes.
Culture: As for *Pilea nummulariifolia.* Must be cut back every spring in order to produce compact plants.
Varieties: 'Silver tree' and 'Nana Bronze'.

Piperaceae

Peperomia argyreia
(Sandersii)   (51)

Rugby Football plant or **Watermelon Peperomia**

Habitat: South America.
Growth: Succulent stems with thick, fleshy, heart-shaped, dark green leaves, which have silvery-white stripes between their curved longitudinal veins. The flowers are gathered into spikes which are like mice tails.
Use: Undemanding indoor plant.
Soil: Soilless mixture.
Feeding: 2 grams of fertiliser per litre ($\frac{1}{2}$ oz. per gallon) of water every 2 weeks (March–September).
Water: Summer, normal watering; winter, keep very dry.

Light: Shade, for example in a window facing north.
Heat: Normal room temperature; will not stand temperatures below minimum 5° C. (40° F.).
Air: Likes a high degree of humidity.
Re-potting: Early spring, in pans. Plant at the same depth as before. Avoid damaging the brittle stems and leaves when re-potting.
Propagation: By leaf cuttings.
Pests: Snails and slugs.
Other species: See below.

Peperomia arifolia

Growth: Pointed, heart-shaped, plain dark green leaves. Many light flower spikes at the tips of the shoots.
Use and culture: As for *Peperomia argyreia.*

Peperomia caperata

Growth: Small, wavy, wrinkled leaves. Dense, firm white flower spike, which is rather like a pipe-cleaner. Flowers both in spring and in autumn, but is not particularly durable indoors.
Culture: As for *Peperomia argyreia.*

Peperomia arifolia

Peperomia caperata

Peperomia griseoargentea

Growth: Silvery-grey, marbled leaves with distinctive veins.
Use and culture: As for *Peperomia argyreia*.

Peperomia obtusifolia   (52)

Growth: Sturdy, dark green leaves, shaped like magnolia leaves with yellowy-white, irregularly distributed spots. The plant may be rejuvenated by stopping in the spring.
Use and culture: As for *Peperomia argyreia*. The 'U.S.A.' variety is to be preferred.

Peperomia subtrinervis   (53)

Growth: Thin, reddish stems with light green leaves. Good hanging plant.
Culture: As for *Peperomia argyreia*.

Piper nigrum

Pepper

Habitat: Malabar Coast.
Growth: Slow-growing, climbing plant with shiny, heart-shaped leaves. The fruits provide black and white pepper, but the flowers do not develop under indoor culture.

Use: Attractive climbing plant in large flower windows.
Soil: Soilless mixture.
Feeding: 2 grams of fertiliser per litre ($\frac{1}{2}$ oz. per gallon) of water every 2 weeks (March–September).
Water: Even watering the whole year round.
Light: Full or half-shade; also thrives in windows facing north.
Heat: Normal room temperatures, but not below minimum 12° C. (55° F.).
Air: Ordinary dry room air.
Re-potting: February, when the new shoots are to be seen.
Propagation: By shoot cuttings over high base heat.
Pests: Red spider mites.
NOTE: White, pearl-like precipitations on the undersides of the leaves are a natural phenomenon and not a sign of disease.

Proteaceae

Grevillea robusta

Habitat: Australia, where the plant is the holy tree of the Aborigines. Here, it grows to a height of 30 m. (nearly 100 ft.) and is the host plant for the epiphytic *Platycerium bifurcatum*.

Piper nigrum

Grevillea robusta

Growth: Slender trunk with light, strongly indented, fern-like leaves.
Use: Best as a 1-year indoor plant in a light window. Older plants grow too big for indoor culture, but are very suitable for conservatories, possibly as tub plants which can be moved out of doors in the summer to be kept on a balcony, on a terrace or in a patio.
Soil: Soilless mixture.
Feeding: 4 grams of fertiliser per litre (1¼ oz. per gallon) of water every 2 weeks (March–September). Winter, no nourishment at all.
Water: Regular watering the whole year round. Both excessive water and extreme drought will damage the roots and may cause the death of the plant.
Light: Will stand large amounts of light. The leaves easily take on a bronzy tinge, however, if exposed to intense sunlight.
Heat: Even warmth the whole year round. Will not stand temperatures which are too high, but on the other hand will not tolerate temperatures below a minimum 15°C. (60°F.).
Air: Dry indoor air.
Re-potting: Early spring, when growth begins.
Propagation: By seed.
Pests: Mealy bug, red spider.

Caryophyllaceae

Dianthus caryophyllus (54)

Carnation

Growth: Sturdy stems with dense leaf rosettes and abundant flowers. Almost all colours are represented in the range of varieties. Delicate fragrance.
Use: Formerly an indoor plant for rooms which were not too warm in the winter. Can be kept in the garden during the summer in a sunny place.
Soil: Soilless mixture, with large amounts of gravel or sand added. Good drainage in the pot.
Feeding: 2 grams of fertiliser per litre (½ oz. per gallon) of water every 3 weeks in the summer-time.
Water: Relatively dry. Never water in the base dish.
Light: Full light, preferably in a sunny spot.
Heat: Out of doors in summer; in winter, best at minimum 12–15°C. (55–60°F.).
Air: Will stand dry air.
Re-potting: The end of summer, after its stay in the garden.
Propagation: By planting cuttings in damp sand as early as possible in the spring, which will produce firm, good flowering plants for September.

Nyctaginaceae

Bougainvillea glabra (55)

Habitat: Brazil.
Growth: Powerful, thorny climbing plant with 3 inconspicuous flowers on each inflorescence, which is surrounded by 3 brightly coloured bracts in red or violet. Flowering in March–July.
Use: Trellis plant for large-scale arrangements, e.g. large flower windows or conservatories. Tub plants can be placed out of doors in a warm spot during the summer.
Soil: Strong garden soil with sand added. (John Innes No. 3.)

Feeding: 2 grams of fertiliser per litre ($\frac{1}{2}$ oz. per gallon) every week (February–September). Has a strong appetite, so alternate indoor plant nourishment with ammonium sulphate.

Water: To be kept well watered during the growth period, but drier in the resting period from September to January.

Light: As sunny as possible.

Heat: Normal temperatures; winter, best at minimum 10–12° C. (50–55° F.).

Air: Spraying when growth begins in the early spring, otherwise dry air.

Re-potting: January, in slightly larger pots. Take care with the thorns.

Propagation: By cuttings in the early spring over strong base heat.

Pests: Scale insects, mealy bug.

NOTE: Flowers are shed with excessive fluctuations in temperature. The lilac form fares best in indoor culture.

Aizoceae

Argyroderma testiculare   (56)

Habitat: South Africa.

Growth: A succulent, the appearance of which tones with the siliceous stone, calcareous tufa and quartz fragments of its surroundings, from which it is difficult to distinguish the plant. At times of rain the plant absorbs large quantities of water, which is stored in cells in the parts which are above the surface and which it uses during the long period of drought. The white, yellow, red or mauve flowers emerge at the beginning of the rainy season which follows, but only unfold properly in full sunshine.

Use: Ideal indoor plant, which 'takes care of itself'. The pot is buried in sand in a box placed in a south-facing window.

Soil: Half sand, half soilless mixture. pH 7·5. Good drainage.

Feeding: Never.

Water: October–February: once every 3 weeks, so that the soil balls do not dry out entirely. March–April: every 3 days, when growth is about to begin. May–September: generous watering in hot weather every day, otherwise as required. Never moisten the plant itself.

Light: Window facing south in direct sunlight.

Heat: Summer, as warm as possible; winter, best at only 6° C. (42° F.). Will not stand frost. Warm winter will cause flowering to fail.

Air: Dry indoor air with sprinkling necessary during summer. Avoid draughts.

Re-potting: Never.

Propagation: By division or seed.

NOTE: Growth is regulated by watering.

Other species: See below.

Conophytum springbokensis   (57)

Growth: Yellow flowers in August. After flowering has ceased the surface of the plant shrivels up and a new pair of leaves develops from the centre.

Culture requirements: Resting period, to be kept warm and dry, April–August. Otherwise, as for *Argyroderma testiculare.*

Faucaria tigrina   (58)

Growth: Edges of the leaves densely covered with sharp 'teeth'. Yellow flowers.

Culture requirements: As for *Argyroderma testiculare.*

Fenestraria rhopalophylla   (59)

Growth: Club-shaped plant with a transparent 'window' at the top, through which the light penetrates to the inner cells of the plant. In nature it will stand being buried in sand as long as the 'window' is kept free.

Culture requirements: As for *Argyroderma testiculare.*

Lithops pseudotruncatella (60)

Growth: Ball-shaped plant with a narrow slit at its centre, from which the flower grows in the summer.

Culture requirements: Should be kept dry in winter and somewhat warmer than *Argyroderma testiculare*, otherwise the same.

Pleiospilos bolusii (61)

Growth: Angular plant with irregularly distributed spots. The flowers are yellow, orange and magenta.

Culture requirements: As for *Argyroderma testiculare*.

In the following descriptions, the term *areole* refers to the area on the leaves (pads) of cactus from which spring spines, bristles, glochids, hairs or wool. *Glochids* are the easily detachable, barbed spines found on many areoles, which are so painful a feature of some cacti, notably *Opuntia* spp.

Cactaceae

Cacti

Habitat: The cactus family covers some 10,000 species, virtually all of them originally from America, mainly the desert regions of Arizona and Mexico, and the Andes Mountains in Bolivia and Peru.

Growth: Cacti make excellent indoor plants. Not least their ability to store water and withstand long periods of drought makes them highly suitable for cultivation in a window. The roots are thick and sturdy and lie just below the surface of the soil, so that pots and dishes should be very flat ones. In nature the root network is able to absorb large quantities of water in a short time during tropical showers, but cannot stand constant moisture. The fleshy stems are designed to convey and store water. Since there are, as a rule, no leaves the

stems assume their functions, providing for evaporation and absorption of carbon dioxide. A layer of wax on the surface skin protects against too much evaporation. Otherwise the stem is protected by the areoles, small patches with tufts of hair, bristles, glochids or spines. Cacti must have reached a certain age before they can flower. The flowers have a dense ring of petals in bright colours which encloses a halo of stamens. The individual flower often has a very short life. The flowers of many types have a delicate, almost soporific fragrance. Certain types have attractive, red, long-lasting soft fruits, others edible fruits.

Use: Cacti are easy indoor plants which require a minimum of attention. They can be cultivated with other succulents, such as *Agave*, *Argyroderma* and *Echeveria*, but, on the other hand, they are difficult with other indoor plants. Every now and then cacti become very fashionable, and the large number of species cultivated make them highly suitable as collector's pieces. All cacti have a number of culture requirements in common, which are described below, while special requirements are indicated under the description of the species concerned.

Soil: Light, porous, half sand, half soilless mixture. pH 6–7. Arrange for efficient drainage in the form of charcoal, shell grit or coarse gravel in the bottom of the pot in order to avoid lingering moisture.

Feeding: Young plants should not be given any nourishment. Older plants: 1 gram of superphosphate + 1 gram of potassium sulphate per litre of water ($\frac{1}{4}$ oz. of each per gallon) every week from June to July. The rest of the year, no nourishment. No nitrogen fertiliser, and no ordinary indoor plant fertiliser containing nitrogen.

Water: November–March: older plants must be kept completely dry. Young plants should be given a little water every 2 weeks, so that they do not become shrivelled. The hotter the environment, the more water is needed. April–May: Let the pot stand deep in water for a few hours, and then allow the water to drip off completely. Subsequently, give calcium-free water (rainwater) once a week. June–October: Water 2–3 times per week, especially in hot and bright weather. Water should also be sprayed over the plant itself, but should not be allowed to remain in the base dish. Place sand or gravel around the neck of the root just at the surface of the soil in order to guard against rot.

Light: As light as possible, preferably full sunlight in a window facing south. Will not thrive on a shelf in a dark room.

Heat: November–March: Best temperature, minimum 6–8° C. (43–46° F.), though some types thrive in temperatures up to 12° C. (54° F.). The hardiest types will survive at ordinary room temperatures, if at the same time they stand in the light and are watered from time to time. April–October: minimum 15–25° C. (60–80° F.).

Air: As dry as possible. Centrally heated air is quite suitable. If left out in the garden during the summer, must be protected by glass or plastic during long periods of rain. Avoid draughts.

Re-potting: Only when the parts above the surface of the soil have filled the pot. Use rubber gloves when re-potting.

Propagation: The seeds of many types can be purchased. Sow during spring or summer in dishes covered by glass or polythene. Cuttings must be taken with a sharp knife, and the cut surface allowed to dry out for a couple of weeks before the cutting is planted into sand. Cacti with many side growths can be propagated by division, possibly at the same time as re-potting. Finally, weaker varieties with small root networks can be grafted on to firmly rooted pillar cacti, best in warm, damp forcing houses or flower windows in June–July. Plants may be handled during trans-

Aporocactus flagelliformis

planting by holding the ends of a paper collar wrapped around the plant.

NOTE: Spines in fingers may be removed with tweezers or by dripping wax from a burning candle on to the wounded spot. The solidified layer of wax will remove the thorn from the skin.

Species: See below.

Aporocactus flagelliformis

Rat-tail Cactus

Habitat: Mexico.

Growth: Long, pendulous shoots, densely covered with small thorns. Large crimson-pink flowers in the spring.

Use: Good indoor plant, best as a hanging plant in a suspended bowl or grafted on to a tall pillar cactus.

Special culture requirements: Must be kept warm and light during winter and not allowed to dry up completely. More water and warmth from February onwards. Concerning culture requirements in general, see *Cacti.*

Cephalocereus senilis

Cephalocereus senilis

Old Man

Habitat: Mexico.
Growth: Slow-growing pillar cactus, densely covered with yellow spines and a thick coat of white, silk-soft hair.
Special culture requirements: Place sand around the root neck, as the roots are weak and rot easily when too much water is given. Will last many years, if it is kept in a light, dry and cool spot. Likes full sunlight in a window facing south. Concerning culture requirements in general, see *Cacti*.
NOTE: Dirty hair can be washed with soapflakes (*not* detergent), provided it is rinsed and dried thoroughly afterwards.

Echinocactus grusonii (62)

Mother-in-law's Chair

Habitat: Mexico.
Growth: Large globe with clearly defined ribs and strong, yellow-gold spines. Young plants have ribs divided into warts, like *Mammillaria hidalgensis*. The small, yellow flowers, which grow in great profusion, are unlikely to be produced except under outdoor tropical conditions or very good greenhouse cultivation.

Special culture requirements: As close as possible to a window facing south. Should spend the winter at minimum 8°C. (45°F.). Must be re-potted frequently and always in the spring. Concerning cultural requirements in general, see *Cacti*.

Echinopsis eyriesii

Habitat: Argentina and Uruguay.
Growth: Globe-shaped, 20 cm. (8 in.) in cross-section. Sharp ribs with white felted areoles bearing sharp spines. Flowers up to 25 cm. (10 in.) long, open, white and fragrant; flowers last only a few hours.
Special culture requirements: Flowering is best attained by removing side shoots. Placed in half-shade during flowering in June–July. During winter must be kept dry at minimum 5°C. (40°F.). Concerning culture requirements in general, see *Cacti*.
NOTE: Has been cultivated for over 200 years. A reliable plant in any cactus collection.

Mamillaria hidalgensis (63)

Habitat: Mexico.
Growth: Globe-cactus with four cross-patterned, attractive spines on wart-like projections, arranged in spiral rows. The flowers are rose-red, the buds developing

Echinopsis eyriesii

Opuntia clavarioides

in the axils—the spaces between the warts—when these have reached a certain age. The flowers are thus always at a certain distance from the centre of the plant. Flowers in summer.
Use: Good indoor plant in full sunlight.
Special culture requirements: Very sensitive to damp soil. Make sure, therefore, that the pot soil is well drained and has a high content of gravel. Protect the root neck against lingering moisture with gravel. To be kept dry at a minimum 8° C. (45° F.) during winter. Concerning culture requirements in general, see *Cacti*.

Opuntia phaeacantha *(form)*   (64)

Habitat: Cool regions in North and South America.
Growth: Round or oval, flat shoots with evenly divided tufts of loosely mounted yellow glochids, bearing pointed barbs which easily attach themselves to clothes and skin. The yellow flowers emerge from the edges of the shoots (pads).
Use: Very suitable for rooms and conservatories.
Special culture requirements: Best at temperatures which are not too high. Can be left to spend the summer in the garden. Concerning culture requirements in general, see *Cacti*.
Other species: See below.

Opuntia clavarioides *(var.* Monstrosa)

Growth: Greenish-brown shoots with white thorns on the crowded areoles. Uneven growth with finger- or hand-shaped protuberances.
Culture requirements: As for *Opuntia phaeacantha*. Can be grafted on to *Opuntia cylindrica*.

Opuntia cylindrica

Growth: Vigorous, tall-growing *Opuntia* species, best for a conservatory.
Culture requirements: As for *Opuntia phaeacantha*.

Opuntia ficus-indica

Prickly Pear

Growth: Vigorous *Opuntia* species, which is used in Southern Europe as an effective hedge plant. When out of control, it is a troublesome weed. The fruit is edible when the glochid-covered skin is removed.
Culture requirements: As for *Opuntia phaeacantha*.

Opuntia tuna

Growth: Vigorous, flat shoots with stiff, yellow-brown spines. Large, pale yellow flowers.
Culture requirements: As for *Opuntia phaeacantha*.

Rebutia minuscula

Habitat: Mountainous regions in Argentina and Bolivia.
Growth: Small globular shape with spiral ribs. Many red flowers, mainly in May.

Rebutia minuscula

Use: Rewarding indoor plant for a window-sill.
Special culture requirements: Winter: very little water, but enough to prevent the plant from drying up. Spring: a lot of water while the buds are forming. Summer: a lot of water, and half-shade. Concerning culture requirements in general, see *Cacti*.

Selenicereus grandiflorus (65)

Night-flowering Cereus

Habitat: Haïti.
Growth: Climbing, many-branched plant; pentagonal, dark green shoots, with short spines and aerial roots on some of the shoots. Large flowers, 30 cm. (12 in.) long and 30 cm. (12 in.) in cross-section, which are golden-brown on the outside and pure white inside. Very delicate fragrance, given off during darkness, and the flower only lasts for a few hours. The plant will not usually flower until it is 8 years old.
Use: Climbing plant in a room or winter garden. Ornamental value, apart from the flower, is debatable.
Special culture requirements: Summer: sunshine, heat, plenty of water and spraying. May, under certain circumstances, be kept out of doors in summer. Winter, minimum 10° C. (50° F.) in a light growth location; water sparingly. Concerning culture requirements in general, see *Cacti*.
Other species: See below.

Selenicereus pteracanthus

Growth: Not as vigorous as *Selenicereus grandiflorus*, but better suited to indoor culture. Flowers during the plant's fifth year of life. Other culture requirements as above.

Schlumbergera gaertneri

Easter Cactus

Habitat: Brazil.
Growth: Very similar, with its flat, segmented, leaf-like shoots, to *Schlumbergera bridgesii*. Continued growth, and the development of buds takes place from a long areole at the tip of each shoot. The flowers are wheel-shaped and brilliant red in colour. Flowering period March–April.
Use: Good indoor plant. Considerably easier to bring to flower than the above-mentioned species. Not sensitive to the pot being turned or moved in the window.
Culture: May–September: Gentle shade, moderate watering, temperature not above minimum 25° C. (80° F.) and frequent spraying. Never direct sunlight. October–November: Cool (minimum 10° C. (50° F.)) and dry in order to promote the formation of buds. December–February: In January the temperature

Schlumbergera gaertneri

Rhipsalis houlletiana

Rhipsalis houlletiana

Habitat: Tropical rain forests in South America.
Growth: Flat, articulated, leaf-like, green shoots, growing up to a metre (3 ft.) in length, with sharp teeth and overhanging growth. The unattractive yellow-green flowers grow in great profusion.
Use: Hanging plant which is grown in small baskets or orchid baskets, as for orchids. Especially good in a conservatory, porch or greenhouse.

can be raised to about 18° C. (65° F.), following which the buds will begin to appear. May–June: Flowering period with somewhat larger amounts of water, temperature about 20° C. (70° F.), and occasional spraying.
Soil: Leaf mould mixed with sand.
NOTE: Shedding segments, attributable as a rule to fluctuating temperature.

Rhipsalidopsis rosea   (66)

Habitat: Brazil.
Growth: Hanging stem with flat, articulated leaf-like shoots around it, like *Schlumbergera bridgesii*. The flowers are large, wheel-shaped and slightly hanging. Varieties with varnish-red, light red and violet flowers. Flowering period March–September.
Use: Suitable for window-sills, or as a hanging-bowl plant. Easier to cultivate, has a lot more flowers than the above-mentioned species.
Culture: Moist, humus-rich soil (soilless mixture). Summer: Evenly moist, light and sunny. During the flowering period, frequent spraying and watering. Winter: Dry and cool (minimum 10° C. (50° F.)). Should be re-potted early in spring, in small pots.

Schlumbergera bridgesii   (67)

Christmas Cactus

Habitat: Tropical rain forests in Brazil.
Growth: Upright or more or less hanging growth. Flat, leaf-like green segments with flowers at their tips. The hanging flowers are dark red with several rings of petals. Frequently grafted on *Selenicereus grandiflorus* in order to develop trunked varieties. The plant's own root network is weak, and will not stand too much water, but must not be allowed to dry out.
Use: Good indoor plant, suitable as a hanging plant. Both *Schlumbergera gaertneri* and *Rhipsalidopsis rosea* are easier, however.
Culture: April–June: Light and moist, but not in direct sunshine. Spraying in hot weather, plenty of water and occasional nourishment. July–August: During the resting period at the height of the summer, the plant must be kept completely dry, in order to promote the development of the buds. September–December: Cool room temperature, best at minimum 15–18° C. (60–65° F.), but not below 12° C. (54° F.); water sparingly but spray frequently. When the buds emerge, give slightly larger amounts of water. The plant must not be moved or turned, and fluctuations in temperature are undesirable. January–

March: After flowering has ceased, 2 months' rest, during which the plant should be kept dry, light and cool (minimum 10°C. (50°F.)).
Soil: Loam mixed with sand most suitable.
NOTE: If allowed to dry out or given too much water, if moved or turned or subjected to excessive temperature fluctuations, the plant may shed its buds.

Epiphyllum hybridum (68)

Habitat: Tropical rain forests in Central and South America.
Growth: Epiphyte with relatively weak roots and flat, leaf-like shoots with tufts of soft needles on the edges. Often short aerial roots in the joints. Flowers are large, white, light red or dark red with a thick tuft of stamens in the centre, and only emerge isolated from the edges of the leaf-branches in April–June.
Use: Easily cultivated indoor plant with no ornamental value outside the flowering season. Can spend the summer out of doors in a shady spot.
Culture: Light and cool growth location, moist soil, plenty of water and spraying in hot weather, also after flowering has ceased. Give plenty of water and weekly application of nourishment until August. Should spend the winter at a minimum 8–12°C. (45–55°F.) and have enough water to avoid shrivelling up of the shoots. High winter temperature promotes the formation of shoots which do not flower and are removed in spring. *Re-potting:* Every 2 or 3 years in light soil, rich in humus (leaf mould with peat or sand added, possibly loamless compost).

Lauraceae

Laurus nobilis

Bay Tree

Growth: Bush or tree with evergreen, coriaceous leaves and small, yellowy-

Laurus nobilis

white flowers. The leaves contain an aromatic flavouring substance.
Use: Tub plant for ornamental purposes. Should spend the winter in a cool, frost-free conservatory, summer out of doors on a terrace or in a patio (April–October).
Soil: Strong, nourishing loam with bonemeal (Animix) added, possibly soil-less mixture.
Feeding: 5 grams of fertiliser per litre (1½ oz. per gallon) of water per week during the growth period.
Water: Plenty during growth period; in winter, just enough to prevent the root mass from drying out altogether.
Light: Will stand some shade. Light during winter.
Heat: Summer, normal temperature; winter, minimum 5°C. (40°F.).
Air: Spraying during the growth period.
Re-potting: Only when the root mass completely fills the tub. Plenty of basic nourishment with weekly additions is preferable to changing the soil.
Pests: Greenfly, mealy-bugs, scale insects.
NOTE: Too much water in the winter will cause yellowing and shedding of leaves.

Passifloraceae
Passiflora coerulea (69)
Passion Flower

Habitat: Central America.
Growth: Climbing plant with palmate leaves, tendrils and strange flower structures, individual parts of which have been associated with items from the story of the Passion of Christ. It is said that the ring of wire-like nectaries is the crown of thorns, the 5 stamens are Christ's wounds, the pistil is the chalice and the triple stigma the nails in the cross. The petals in the white variety symbolise the Saviour's innocence, and the petals of the blue variety take their colour from the Virgin Mary's sky blue cloak. Flowering period is July–September. The single flower only lasts for a day; the fruit is pretty and edible.
Use: Attractive climbing plant in a light window or a conservatory, or in a warm spot out of doors. May be cultivated as an annual or perennial plant, though it will not flower the same year as seed is sown.
Soil: Strong garden soil with bonemeal added. Not soilless mixture.
Feeding: 3 grams of fertiliser per litre (1 oz. per gallon) of water, every week April–September.
Water: Plenty during the summer; in winter, only a little, but the soil should not be allowed to dry out completely.
Light: Very demanding, but should be slightly shaded from scorching midday sun.
Heat: Moderate temperature; winter, best at minimum 8° C. (45° F.).
Air: Damp air at the beginning of growth in spring.
Re-potting: Early spring, before the new shoots develop.
Cutting: In spring the flowering shoots of the previous year are cut back, down to 6–8 buds.
Propagation: By layers, cuttings and seeds.

Pests: Red spider mites.
Varieties: 'Constance Elliott' (white) and 'Empress Eugenie'(violet).
Other species: See below.

Passiflora coccinea

Growth: Small, red star flowers.
Use and culture: As for *Passiflora coerulea.* Winter temperature minimum 10–12° C. (50–55° F.).

Passiflora racemosa

Growth: Red flowers in small clusters.
Use and culture: As for *Passiflora coerulea.*

Begoniaceae
Begonia cheimantha
(B. socotrana × B. dregei) (70)
'Gloire de Lorraine'

Growth: Dense plant with succulent, fragile roots, light green leaves and white, pale red and plain red flowers in great profusion.
Use: Originally, a distinct Christmas bloom, which is now cultivated from the early autumn to late spring. Cheap and easy ornamental plant which, with good care, will last for many years in indoor culture. Cut flowers are highly ornamental, and last a long time in water.
Soil: Soilless mixture, possibly half garden soil and half peat. pH 7.
Feeding: 1 gram of fertiliser per litre ($\frac{1}{4}$ oz. per gallon) of water, every week during the growth period.
Water: The pot soil should be kept evenly moist. Best watered through a base dish; excess water should be poured away half an hour after watering. When watered too sparingly, buds and flowers are shed.
Light: Likes a light spot but away from direct sunshine.
Heat: Should be gradually accustomed

Begonia socotranum x tuberhybrida

to room temperature, from minimum 12°C. (55°F.) in October to minimum 18°C. (65°F.) in mid-winter. Higher temperatures cause dropping of flowers and prevent the development of new buds.

Air: Fresh air counteracts attack from mildew.

Re-potting: Re-pot older plants carefully, when the roots fill the pots.

Cutting: After flowering has ceased, cut back the top so that the plant can flower again.

Propagation: By cuttings in a forcing house.

Diseases: Mildew, especially in still, damp air. Shedding of buds and flowers when soil is too dry and temperature too high.

Varieties: 'Marina' (pink), 'Marietta' (pink) and 'Regent' (pale pink).

Other species: See below.

Begonia socotrana tuberhybrida

Growth: Smaller than *Begonia cheimantha*, but has larger flowers. Use and culture otherwise the same.

Varieties: 'Elatior' (crimson), 'Baardses Favorite' (bright red), 'President' (red, double), 'Oranje Zon' (orange) and 'Exquisite' (pink).

Begonia rex-cultorum   (71)

Growth: Short, downy stems and leaves on long stalks with attractive patterns. Small, dirty-white flowers in clusters, February–April. Found in a large variety of types and hybrids with different leaf patterns in red, silvery-grey and green.

Use: Long-lasting indoor plant.

Soil: Soilless mixture.

Feeding: 2 grams of fertiliser per litre ($\frac{1}{2}$ oz. per gallon) of water every week, February–September.

Water: Water evenly but sparingly during the resting period from October to January.

Light: Half-shade, never direct sunshine.

Heat: Normal room temperature (approx. 20°C. (70°F.)). Sensitive to temperatures below 10°C. (50°F.).

Air: Damp air with frequent spraying in the spring.

Re-potting: After flowering has ceased in May.

Propagation: By leaf cuttings.

Begonia argenteo-guttata

Pests: Thrips in dry environments, red spider mites in sunlight.

Begonia argenteo-guttata

Growth: Creeping, succulent, downy stems. The wing-shaped leaves are bronze-coloured with silvery-grey markings. Pink flowers in hanging inflorescences.
Use: Good indoor plant in a warm room, conservatory or hothouse.
Culture: As for *Begonia rex-cultorum*.
Other species of fibrous-rooted begonia: See below.

Begonia corallina

Growth: Shiny leaves with red undersides. Coral red, hanging flowers.
Use and culture: As for *Begonia rex-cultorum*. Needs a lot of warmth.
Hybrids: A good hybrid is 'President Carnot', with tall, robust stems, reddish leaves with white markings and crimson flower clusters.

Begonia credneri

Growth: Vigorous growth. Downy, olive-green leaves with dark patterns.

Begonia corallina

Begonia fuchsioides

Light red flowers in large clusters the whole year round.
Use and culture: As for *Begonia rex-cultorum*. Will stand more sunlight than the other Begonias.
Varieties: 'Berlin', 'Dresden' and 'Stuttgart' with downy leaves having red undersides, and white flowers.

Begonia erythrophylla

Growth: The leaves are wax-like and olive-green with red undersides. The flowers are a delicate pink in the winter.
Use and culture: As for *Begonia rex-cultorum*. Will stand ordinary room temperatures.

Begonia fuchsioides

Growth: Branched, slightly pendulous stems. Leaves are a glistening dark green. Pink flowers in summer and autumn.
Use and culture: As for *Begonia rex-cultorum*. Will stand ordinary room temperatures.

Begonia manicata

Begonia manicata

Growth: Has rosettes of red down on stems and at base of leaves. Tall stems with pale pink flower clusters in the winter.

Use and culture: As for *Begonia rex-cultorum*.

Begonia masoniana 'Iron Cross'

Growth: Tough, embossed leaves with dark patterns like 'iron crosses'. Older leaves are silvery-grey with red down. The flowers are greenish-white with red down.

Use and culture: As for *Begonia rex-cultorum*.

Begonia semperflorens

Growth: Low compact plant with small white, pink or red flowers the whole year round.

Use: For planting out in a flower-bed or a balcony-box, but also suitable as an indoor plant in not too warm a room.

Soil: Soilless mixture.

Feeding: 3 grams of fertiliser per litre of water (1 oz. per gallon) every week (February–November).

Water: Normal watering the whole year round.

Light: Will stand sunshine, but should be slightly shaded in the height of the summer.

Heat: Fares best at minimum 12–15° C. (55–60° F.).

Air: Will stand very dry room air.

Re-potting: Spring, when the roots fill the pot.

Cutting: Prune tops when flowering is too meagre.

Propagation: By seeding.

Varieties: 'Harzperle', 12 cm. (4 in.) tall, pink flowers, red leaves; 'Pandy', 12 cm. (4 in.) tall, red; 'Tausendschön', 15 cm. (5 in.) tall, pink and white variant; 'Carmen', 20 cm. (8 in.) tall, plain pink; 'Albert Martin', 35 cm. (13 in.) tall, purple-red.

Begonia tuberhybrida (72)

Growth: Thick, flat tubers, slanted leaves and large numbers of single or double flowers in shades of white, yellow, orange and red.

Use: Primarily a summer flower for the garden, balcony-box or flower-bowl, but can also be cultivated as a summer-flowering indoor plant in light and airy windows.

Soil: Soilless mixture.

Begonia semperflorens

Feeding: 2 grams of fertiliser per litre ($\frac{1}{2}$ oz. per gallon) of water every 2 weeks (April–August).

Water: The soil balls must not be allowed to dry out. The dry tuber should be kept in dry peat litter or sand during the winter.

Light: Window facing south.

Heat: Normal room temperature.

Air: Fresh, not too damp.

Re-potting: The tuber is potted in February for forcing at even heat.

Propagation: By seeding or side tubers. (Cuttings are quite easy.)

Disease: Mildew.

Varieties: There are a large number of varieties, single or double, in many bright colours, for example, 'Frau Helene Harms' (yellow), 'Flamboyant' (red) and 'Pendula' (red), the last-mentioned being a hanging plant and suitable for a suspended basket.

Theaceae

Camellia japonica (73)

Habitat: Mountain forests in Eastern Asia.

Growth: Branching bush with attractive coriaceous leaves and large, single or double flowers in white, pink or red.

Use: Excellent plant in cool conservatories or unheated but frost-free verandas. Only successful as an indoor plant if it is kept constantly in the same place and not turned.

Soil: Soilless mixture or lime-free loam with peat and sand added. Good drainage.

Feeding: 2 grams of ammonium sulphate, alternated with 2 grams normal plant fertiliser per litre ($\frac{1}{2}$ oz. per gallon in each case) of water every 2 weeks, January–July.

Water: The amount of moisture in the pot soil should be kept constant the whole time, but the soil must never be thoroughly wet. Only use rainwater or some other soft water, or add 2 parts per

Oxalis deppei

thousand of ammonium sulphate to normal tap water on each watering.

Light: Light window facing east or west, without direct, scorching midday sun.

Heat: Buds form best in January at minimum 18° C. (65° F.). When the buds are large and swollen, the temperature should be reduced to minimum 8° C. (46° F.) for a few weeks. The flowers emerge when the plant is replaced in a warm environment (minimum 15° C. (60° F.)). Summer, normal room temperature; from October to December, cooler once more (minimum 8° C. (46° F.)).

Air: Damp air, especially while buds are forming. Spray daily.

Re-potting: After flowering has ceased in the early summer.

Propagation: By cuttings or grafting in specialised nurseries.

Diseases: Bud drop is caused by excessive heat, temperature fluctuations, too much soil moisture (or excessive dryness) or removal of the plant.

Oxalidaceae

Oxalis deppei

Habitat: Mexico.

Growth: Tuberous, edible rhizomes, four-bladed, clover-like leaves with dark ribbon patterns and tile-red flowers.

Use: Undemanding indoor plant.
Soil: Soilless mixture.
Feeding: 2 grams of fertiliser per litre ($\frac{1}{2}$ oz. per gallon) of water every 2 weeks (March–August).
Water: Plenty during growth period, very sparing during the resting period in the winter.
Light: Window facing east or west.
Heat: Normal room temperature.
Air: Dry room air.
Re-potting: Early spring.
Propagation: By side tubers, which are separated from the parent plant at the same time as re-potting.

Geraniaceae

Pelargonium × domesticum (74)

Regal Pelargonium

Growth: Low, branching bush with sharp-toothed, downy leaves. Large, white, pink or red flowers with spots, veins or flames in various colours, collected into round inflorescences. Flowers during the whole of the summer.
Use: Perennial plant with cool wintering on a light veranda, in a conservatory or other such unheated, frost-free indoor location. May also be used out of doors in a balcony box or plant tub during the summer. The plant is most attractive, and flowers most abundantly in its third year.
Soil: Soilless mixture or other soil rich in nutrients. pH 5–6·5.
Feeding: 5 grams of fertiliser per litre ($1\frac{1}{2}$ oz. per gallon) of water every week (April–August).
Water: Plenty during growth period; resting period from August, with less water. When the new shoots begin to develop in September, start to water generously once more. From November, very dry, cool winter.
Light: As much as possible. During flowering, best placed in a window facing east or west.

Heat: Normal room temperature; winter, minimum 8° C. (45° F.).
Air: Fresh, not enclosed and not too dry.
Re-potting: Early spring, before growth begins.
Cutting: Pruning after flowering has ceased in August, so as to favour the growth of vigorous bushy plants.
Propagation: Pruned top shoots can be used as cuttings, which are planted in moist, plain sand.
Pest: Greenfly.
Disease: Fungus on leaves is as a rule due to lack of fresh air.
Varieties: 'Frühlingszauber' (pale pink/reddish brown); 'Schneewittchen' (white/carmine); 'Glut' (cherry-red/white/black spots).

Pelargonium × hortorum (75)

Geranium

Habitat: South Africa.
Growth: Upright stems with round green leaves having a brown horseshoe pattern. Self-coloured flowers (white, pink, mauve and red varieties) in dense inflorescences.
Use: Good plant for balcony boxes or bowls out of doors in summer. Otherwise undemanding, perennial indoor plant, best kept cool during winter on a veranda, in a conservatory or similar. Easily satisfied plant in a warm sunny window facing south.
Soil: Soilless mixture.
Feeding: 5 grams of fertiliser per litre ($1\frac{1}{2}$ oz. per gallon) of water every week from March to August.
Water: Summer: Normal watering. Will stand being kept dry for a time. Winter: Dry.
Light: Will stand direct sunlight. Plenty of light in winter.
Heat: Normal room temperature; winter, minimum 10° C. (50° F.).
Air: Fresh, not enclosed air.
Re-potting: Early spring, before growth begins.

Cutting: Late summer, after flowering has ceased.

Propagation: By cuttings from summer pruning, or cuttings from the new growth in early spring.

Varieties: 'Volkskanzler' (bright red), 'Zink' (deep red), 'Åvang' (salmon red).

Pelargonium peltatum (76)
Ivy-leafed Geranium

Growth: Metre-long (3-ft.) hanging stems with elegant, ivy-like leaves. Large influorescences in white, pink, mauve and red. One or two double varieties.

Use: Good balcony plant. Indoor hanging-bowl plant for a room or conservatory. Not a climber.

Soil: Soilless mixture, possibly with gravel or sand added.

Feeding: 3 grams of fertiliser per litre (1 oz. per gallon) of water every week during the growth period.

Water: Water normally in summer, sparingly in winter.

Light: Full sunlight.

Heat: Summer, humid, around minimum 20° C. (70° F.), winter about minimum 10° C. (50° F.).

Air: Absolutely fresh, but will stand dry room air.

Re-potting: Early spring.

Cutting: After flowering has ceased, and before the winter resting period begins.

Propagation: By cuttings in the late summer.

Varieties: 'Balkonkönigin' (pale pink), 'Jeanne d'Arc' (white), 'Cattleya' (mauve), 'M. Marquis' (red).

Balsaminaceae

Impatiens walleriana (77)
Busy Lizzie

Habitat: Tropical Africa.

Growth: Herbaceous, succulent stems with fresh green leaves and single, flat flowers in white, pale red or scarlet.

Use: Undemanding, immensely prolific indoor flower plant. Suitable for outdoor use in the summer in a balcony box, on a terrace or in a patio.

Soil: Soilless mixture.

Feeding: 3 grams of fertiliser per litre (1 oz. per gallon) of water each week (February–September). Flowering will be too meagre if insufficient nourishment is given.

Water: Heavy consumption; during the hot season, frequently needs to be watered several times a day. In winter, water more sparingly.

Light: Light shade during the summer, not direct sunshine. Light during the winter.

Heat: Normal room temperature. Very warm during the winter (minimum 20° C. (70° F.)) in a light location; then cooler (minimum 12° C. (55° F.)) with a shadier position.

Air: Humid air. Spraying needed.

Re-potting: Early spring. Vigorous plants possibly again in June.

Cutting: Top pruning after each major flowering. The plant rapidly spreads new shoots and many flower buds.

Propagation: By cuttings of pruned top shoots, which easily strike roots in water.

Pests: Greenfly, red spider mites.

NOTE: One of our most prolific flowering indoor plants.

Rutaceae

Fortunella japonica (78)
Kumquat

Habitat: China.

Growth: Small tree with shiny leaves, small, white, fragrant flowers, and small orange-yellow, long-lasting fruits, which are edible but very bitter.

Use: The orange and lemon trees grown in the South grow indoors well enough but can rarely, if ever, be brought to flower or bear fruit. On the other hand, the Chinese Kumquat is an excellent plant for light windows, where it flowers almost the whole year round and at the same time bears long-lasting miniature oranges.

Soil: Soilless mixture.
Feeding: 2 grams of fertiliser per litre ($\frac{1}{2}$ oz. per gallon) of water every 2 weeks (February–October).
Water: Plenty, but allow the soil to dry out between times.
Light: Full sunlight.
Heat: Normal room temperature; winter, not below minimum 10° C. (50° F.).
Air: Will stand dry room air.
Re-potting: Frequent re-potting, as growth proceeds rapidly.
Cutting: Prune back top shoots, if the plant begins to take up too much of the window.
Propagation: By top cuttings over bottom heat.
NOTE: The seeds of oranges, lemons and grapefruit can be sown in window-pots, where they quickly germinate and will make attractive, evergreen miniature plants, but—as a rule—they are unable to flower, still less bear fruit.

Tiliaceae

Sparmannia africana   (79)

African Hemp

Habitat: Africa.
Growth: Vigorous plant with lime-like, downy leaves and off-white flowers with yellow and dark red stamens. The flowering period occurs in the spring and summer.
Use: Indoor plant for large-scale requirements, e.g. a veranda or conservatory. Cannot spend the summer out of doors, since the soft leaves are destroyed in windy weather.
Soil: Soilless mixture (large pots).
Feeding: 3 grams of fertiliser per litre (1 oz. per gallon) of water every week (March–September).
Water: Plenty during the growth period; water more sparingly in winter.

Light: Full sunlight.
Heat: Summer, normal room temperature; winter, minimum 12° C. (55° F.).
Air: Will stand dry room air.
Re-potting: February, in large pots on account of the vigorous root network.
Propagation: By firm top shoots in the spring.
Pest: Red spider mite (yellow leaf spots).
Disease: Leaves turn yellow and drop when insufficient nourishment is given.

Malvaceae

Abutilon hybridum

Habitat: South America.
Growth: Small bush with 3–5 lobed leaves shaped like maple leaves. There are varieties with variegated yellow leaves. The flowers are hanging bells with conspicuous yellow stamens and pistil in · the middle. They appear throughout the summer, in colours including white, yellow and dark purple.
Use: Good indoor plant in rooms which are not too warm. Suitable for conservatories and verandas, and in the summer for warm terraces or patios.
Soil: Soilless mixture.
Feeding: 3 grams of fertiliser per litre (1 oz. per gallon) of water every week (February–August).
Water: Summer, plenty; in winter, simply keep the soil slightly damp.
Light: Half-shade in summer; winter, light.
Heat: Normal room temperature; winter, about 15° C. (60° F.) minimum.
Air: Spraying in spring, otherwise dry room air.
Re-potting: April, in pots which are not too large. Add basic nourishment (e.g. bonemeal, Peraform) when re-potting.
Cutting: Trim large plants by hard pruning in April.
Propagation: Pruned top shoots are rooted in damp sand.
Pests: Greenfly in dry air and draughts,

red spider mites in too sunny growth locations.

Diseases: Sudden changes in temperature cause leaves to turn yellow and fall.

Other species: See below.

Abutilon megapotamicum (80)
Brazilian Abutilon

Growth: Small leaves, overhanging branches and yellow and red lantern flowers. The *aureum* form has variegated yellow foliage.

Use and culture: As for *Abutilon hybridum.*

Abutilon striatum thompsonii (81)
Thompson's Abutilon

Growth: Orange-red flowers and variegated yellow foliage.

Use and culture: As for *Abutilon hybridum.*

Hibiscus rosa-sinensis (82)
Hibiscus

Habitat: Tropics.

Growth: Dense bush with fresh green foliage and very large funnel-shaped flowers with yellow pistils and stamens.

Colours: White, yellow, pink and red. Double forms may be found. The individual flower only lasts for a few days.

Use: Good prolific indoor flower plant for light, but not warm, rooms. May be left on a warm balcony or in a similar outdoor location during the summer.

Soil: Soilless mixture.

Feeding: 3 grams of fertiliser per litre (1 oz. per gallon) of water, every week (February–August).

Water: Plenty during the summer, somewhat less in winter, but never allow to dry out completely.

Light: Half-shade in summer, preferably in a window facing north. As light as possible in winter for early flowering.

Heat: Normal room temperature; winter, not less than 12° C. (55° F.). Fares best at minimum 20° C. (70° F.).

Malvastrum capense

Air: Slightly humid air. The leaves roll up in excessively dry air and buds are shed.

Re-potting: February.

Cutting: Prune older, larger plants in February.

Propagation: By top cuttings from pruned material.

Pests: Greenfly, mealy bugs, red spider mites.

Diseases: Changing temperature and air humidity cause shedding of buds.

Malvastrum capense

Habitat: South Africa.

Growth: Small bush with downy, slightly sticky, 3-lobed leaves, rather like those of a gooseberry bush. The flowers are small, pink and mallow-like.

Use: Good flowering indoor plant.

Culture: As for *Abutilon hybridum.* Grows thin and scraggy in shade. Will stand being thoroughly pruned in the spring.

Euphorbiaceae

Acalypha hispida

Habitat: Tropics.

Growth: Shrubby plant with green leaves and long red inflorescences,

Acalypha hispida

shaped like a cat's tail. Young plants with a single growth provide the biggest inflorescences.

Use: Attractive indoor plant in spring and summer. Difficult plant to bring through the winter.
Soil: Soilless mixture.
Feeding: 2 grams of fertiliser per litre ($\frac{1}{2}$ oz. per gallon) of water every 2 weeks (February–August).
Water: Evenly moist, but not too wet.
Light: Window facing east or west, not direct sunshine.
Heat: As warm as possible. Certainly not below 15° C. (60° F.).
Air: Very damp air. In central heating, the leaves roll up.
Re-potting: February, in small pots.
Cutting: The top shoots on older plants should be cut back to obtain a better spread of branches.
Propagation: By cuttings over high bottom heat.
Pests: Red spider mites in dry air.
Other species: See below.

Acalypha wilkesiana

Growth: Foliage plant with attractively marbled leaves in plain red, copper-red

and brown colours. The flowers are not worthy of special comment. There are many hybrids.
Use and culture: As for *Acalypha hispida*.

Codiaeum variegatum (83)

Croton

Habitat: India. (East Indies.)
Growth: Evergreen bush with a wide variety of leaf-shapes and colours in green, yellow, orange and red shades.
Use: Typical tropical plant, which likes a high temperature and a high degree of air humidity. Best in a hot greenhouse or conservatory. Not so well suited for rooms with dry air. Can be used as an ornamental plant for short periods.
Soil: Soilless mixture.
Feeding: 3 grams of fertiliser per litre (1 oz. per gallon) of water every 2 weeks (March–August).
Water: Normal watering. Should not have too much moisture, but should not be allowed to dry out completely.
Light: Window facing east or west, not direct sunshine. When strongly shaded the leaves turn green and lose their coloured patterns altogether.
Heat: High room temperature; winter, not below minimum 18° C. (65° F.).
Air: High degree of air humidity the whole year round. Frequent spraying.
Re-potting: February.
Cutting: Nipping the top shoots produces bushy plants.
Propagation: By cuttings over high base heat, in February.
Pests: Red spider mites, thrips, scale insects, mealy-bugs.
Diseases: Leaves are shed when the plant is subjected to sudden changes in temperature.

Euphorbia pulcherrima (84)

Poinsettia

Habitat: Mexico.
Growth: Branching bush with slightly

indented leaves. Small, yellowy-green flowers surrounded by a ring of bright red bracts. When cut or damaged the plant exudes a milky substance, known as latex.

Use: Seasonal plant which is sold around Christmas-time, and with care will prove an excellent perennial indoor plant. If kept in the dark for 14 hours out of every 24 during 4 weeks, flowering can be induced at any season of the year.

Soil: Soilless mixture, possibly with the addition of extra bonemeal as basic fertiliser.

Feeding: 3 grams of fertiliser per litre (1 oz. per gallon) of water every week (June–October). (Has a large appetite.)

Water: Plenty during the summer, and always lukewarm, never cold tap water. After flowering and until the May resting period, give less water by comparison. The soil must, however, not be allowed to dry out, otherwise the leaves will be shed.

Light: Summer, half-shade, otherwise as light as possible so that colour is obtained on the bracts.

Heat: Normal room temperature. Flowering plants last longest at minimum 15° C. (60° F.).

Air: Best in damp air. Frequent spraying.

Re-potting: In May the old soil is shaken loose from the roots, the top is cut back and the plant is re-potted in pots which are not too large. Bleeding wounds on branches may be stopped by steeping in warm water.

Propagation: By cuttings in sand and peat at minimum 20° C. (70° F.) in late summer.

Pests: Red spider mites.

Varieties: 'Paul Mikkelsen' (dark red, very long-lasting), 'Annette Hogg' (dark red, many branches), 'Mikkelpink' and 'Middeldawn' (pale red), 'Mikkelwhite' and 'White Ecke' (white).

Other species: See below. Most Euphorbias (Spurges) are decorative and undemanding indoor plants, suitable for cultivation in sunny windows in dry air. There are a number of succulent varieties to choose from. Globe-shaped, or pillar-shaped, with or without cactus-like thorns, with or without green foliage leaves.

Euphorbia milii (85)

Crown of Thorns

Habitat: Madagascar.

Growth: Slightly twining, angular, grey-green branches, densely covered with long, pointed thorns. Fresh-green foliage leaves. Coral-red bracts together with small, greenish-yellow flowers in the spring.

Use: First-class indoor plant in baking hot sunshine in a south-facing position. Very slow growth.

Soil: Soilless mixture.

Feeding: 2 grams of fertiliser per litre ($\frac{1}{2}$ oz. per gallon) every 2 weeks (April–August).

Water: No water, January–February. A little water on sunny days in March. The rest of the year, moderate watering. The soil should be left to dry out between each watering.

Light: Full sunlight.

Heat: Normal room temperature. Will also stand a cool winter at minimum 12° C. (55° F.).

Air: Will stand both dry and damp air.

Re-potting: At intervals of several years. Take care with the thorns.

Cutting: May–June, to obtain the best branch formation.

Propagation: By cuttings from older shoots. The cut surface must be allowed to dry in the air before grafting into equal parts of sand and soil.

Diseases: Leaf shedding is a sign of too low temperatures or too much moisture.

NOTE: Leaf shedding during the resting period is normal, and new leaves appear when the new growth period begins. Apparently dead plants are still alive if the actual shoot tips are green.

Euphorbia erythraea

Euphorbia pugniformis (86)

Habitat: South Africa.
Growth: Succulent with white milk-sap. Snake-like side shoots spread out on all sides from the plant's globular central growth, covered with small yellow flowers. The side shoots last one year, wither and are replaced by new 'tentacles'. The plant in its entirety is 10 cm. (4 in.) high.
Use: Rewarding indoor plant, even in a dry centrally heated atmosphere.
Soil: Soilless mixture or cactus soil (see p. 194) with good drainage. Deep pots on account of the long roots.
Feeding: 3 grams of fertiliser per litre (1 oz. per gallon) of water every 3 weeks (April–June).
Water: Moderate with complete drying out between each watering. Winter, very little water. Avoid applying water directly on to the plant.
Light: A lot of light, preferably full sunlight.
Heat: Summer, normal temperature. Winter, not below minimum 15° C. (60° F.).
Air: Dry room air.
Re-potting: February.
Propagation: By cuttings into plain sand.

Euphorbia canariensis

Habitat: Canary Islands.
Growth: Columnar, thorny stems, which only branch at ground level.
Use and culture: As for *Euphorbia pugniformis.*

Euphorbia erythraea

Growth: High, candelabra-like, thorny stems, covered with small, green foliage leaves, which are shed during growth.
Use and culture: As for *Euphorbia pugniformis.* Will stand temperatures of minimum 18–20° C. (65–70° F.) in winter.

Euphorbia obesa

Habitat: South Africa, where the plant is protected.
Growth: Globular stems, with deep ridges which give the plant the appearance of a fossilised sea urchin.
Use and culture: As for *Euphorbia pugniformis.* Easy to propagate from seeds.

Euphorbia ramipressa

Growth: Flat, antler-like stems. Requires a large amount of space breadthwise.
Use and culture: As for *Euphorbia pugniformis.*

Euonymus japonicus

NOTE: Bleeding from wounds in lacerated stems can be stopped by squirting with warm water.

Euphorbia schimperi

Growth: Slender, smooth, succulent stems, almost without foliage leaves.
Use and culture: As for *Euphorbia pugniformis*. Requires the minimum of attention.

Euphorbia undulatifolia

Growth: Stubby, round, smooth stems and oleander-like, hanging leaves.
Use and culture: As for *Euphorbia pugniformis*.

Celastraceae
Euonymus japonicus

Habitat: Japan.
Growth: Evergreen bush with coriaceous, green leaves and unattractive white flowers in great profusion. Variants can be found with leaves variegated with yellow or white.
Use: Tub plant for conservatories and verandas. Can be left out of doors in the summer, but only in a warm spot.
Soil: Heavy, nourishing garden soil with bonemeal added as basic fertiliser.
Feeding: 5 grams of fertiliser per litre ($1\frac{1}{2}$ oz. per gallon) of water every 2 weeks (April–August).
Water: Summer, plenty; winter, moderate amounts, but the soil must not be allowed to dry out completely.
Light: Full or half-shade.
Heat: Normal temperature. Winter, protected from frost, but preferably at a minimum 5° C. (40° F.).
Air: Summer, damp air; winter, dry.
Re-potting: Every other spring in tubs which are not too small.
Cutting: Trim back young shoots in order to form the plant.
Propagation: By cuttings of mature shoots in the spring.

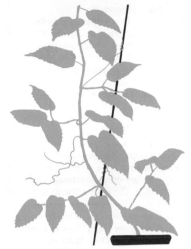

Cissus antarctica

Pests: Mealy bugs, scale insects.
Diseases: Mildew if exposed to too much dampness in winter.

Vitaceae
Cissus antarctica
Kangaroo Vine

Habitat: Australia.
Growth: Vigorous climbing plant, with shiny, oval, serrated leaves.
Use: Shade-plant for windows facing north, or possibly east or west, as long as there is not direct sunlight.
Soil: Light garden soil mixed with sand without peat.
Feeding: 4 grams of fertiliser per litre ($1\frac{1}{4}$ oz. per gallon) of water every week (March–August). Never feed during the dark season.
Water: Moderate amounts. Sensitive to too much moisture, especially in winter.
Light: Slight shade; never direct sunlight.
Heat: Cool spot; winter best at minimum 15° C. (60° F.). Never place above a radiator.

Air: Normal room air.
Re-potting: Every year in February.
Cutting: Stopping young shoots fosters the development of side shoots.
Propagation: By cuttings in April–May.
Diseases: Brown spots on leaves are the result of too much light or moisture.
Other species: See below.

Cissus discolor

Habitat: Java.
Growth: Hanging shoots with attractive heart-shaped, olive-green leaves; these have silvery-grey marbling, and red undersides. The young leaves are violet-purple.
Use and culture: Hanging-bowl plant, which requires high temperature and very humid air. Only suitable for warm conservatories. Otherwise, the same as for *Cissus antarctica*.

Cissus striata

Habitat: Japan.
Growth: Richly branching, climbing plant with small, 5-fingered leaves.
Use and culture: Hanging-bowl or trellis plant in slightly shaded windows at normal room temperature. Otherwise, the same as for *Cissus antarctica*.

Cissus discolor

Cissus striata

Parthenocissus henryana

Habitat: China.
Growth: Deciduous climbing plant with metre-long (3-ft.) shoots. The leaves are moss-green with silvery-white veins and reddish-violet undersides.
Use: Suitable as a climbing plant with the trails tied to a small wire or bamboo trellis, or as a hanging-bowl plant with trails hanging freely.
Soil: Soilless mixture.
Feeding: 4 grams of fertiliser per litre ($\frac{1}{4}$ oz. per gallon) of water every week (April–July).
Water: Give enough but in moderate amounts. Winter, relatively dry.
Light: Half-shade.
Heat: Temperatures should not be too high. Winter, around minimum 8° C. (45° F.).
Air: Dry air.
Re-potting: February.
Cutting: Prune hard on re-potting.
Propagation: By cuttings of mature wood in February.
NOTE: No leaves during the 6-month winter season.

Rhoicissus rhomboidea

Natal Vine

Habitat: South Africa.
Growth: Vigorous climbing plant with
trifoliate, glistening green leaves, the
undersides of which are covered with
brown down.
Use and culture: Suitable for a half-dark
room or for a window facing north. Requires a lot of space. A more rewarding
indoor plant than *Cissus antarctica*.
Culture otherwise the same.
Varieties: 'Jubilee', with larger, coriaceous leaves and slower growth. Very
long-lasting indoors.

Tetrastigma voinierianum

Habitat: Asia.
Growth: Very vigorous climbing plant
with large leaves, consisting of 5 leaflets,
which are reminiscent of the foliage of a
horse-chestnut tree. Trails and young
leaves are covered with reddish-brown
down.
Use: Trellis plant requiring a large
amount of space. Good ornamental
plant for conservatories, halls, vestibules and stairways.
Soil: Soilless mixture.
Feeding: 5 grams of fertiliser per litre

Tetrastigma voinierianum

($1\frac{1}{2}$ oz. per gallon) of water every week
(March–August).
Water: Plenty in summer, allowing the
soil to dry out in between times. Winter,
very dry.
Light: Half-shade, no direct sunlight.
Heat: Cool room; winter, minimum 10–
15° C. (50–60° F.).
Air: Dry indoor air. Spray during the
spring.
Re-potting: March, in pots which are
not too small.
Tying up: Plenty of space between the
trails, so that the large leaves have
freedom to develop.
Propagation: By cuttings in February.
Pests: Red spider mites, mealy bugs.
Diseases: Yellow leaves with too little
nourishment.

Crassulaceae

Aeonium arboreum

Habitat: Canary Islands.
Growth: Trunked, branching succulent
with flat leaf rosette.
Use: May be cultivated in a sunny
window along with cacti, euphorbias
and other succulents. May be left out of
doors for the summer if in a warm spot.

Rhoicissus rhomboidea

Aeonium arboreum

Soil: Soilless mixture, with good drainage.
Feeding: 2 grams of fertiliser per litre ($\frac{1}{2}$ oz. per gallon) of water every 2 weeks (April–August).
Water: Summer, normal watering; winter, completely dry.
Light: Full sunlight.
Heat: Normal temperature; winter minimum 8° C. (46° F.).
Air: Dry indoor air.
Re-potting: Seldom necessary.
Propagating: By cuttings of side shoots in the spring.
Diseases: Rot and mildew can be caused by too much moisture in winter.
Variant: foliis-purpureis, with purple leaves.
Other species: See below.

Aeonium tabuliforme

Growth: Flat, plate-like rosette with dense leaves.
Use and culture: As for *Aeonium arboreum*.

Bryophyllum daigremontianum (87)

Habitat: Madagascar.
Growth: Succulent with oblong-pointed leaves with brown spots. In the inner indentations of the leaf edge, numerous plantlets develop in the form of small rosettes with fine roots. These small plants are subsequently released and fall to the ground, where they immediately strike roots. Pink flowers on a 30-cm. (12-in.)-high stem.
Use: Good indoor plant for light windows.
Soil: Soilless mixture.
Feeding: 3 grams of fertiliser per litre (1 oz. per gallon) every 3 weeks (May–August).
Water: Summer, normal watering; winter, almost dry.
Light: Sunlight.
Heat: Normal temperature; winter, best at minimum 12° C. (55° F.).
Air: Dry air.
Re-potting: Has a tendency to form long, leggy plants, thus rejuvenation by growing on the plantlets is worth while.
Propagation: By potting plantlets once they have fallen, in soil mixed with sand.
Pests: Slugs and snails.
Other species: See below.

Bryophyllum tubiflorum (88)

Growth: Thick, rod-shaped leaves with plantlets at their tips. The structure is somewhat like that of a horsetail or a conifer. The leaves are grey-green with

Cotyledon undulata

Crassula lactea

darker spots, the flowers orange-yellow in colour.
Use and culture: As for *Bryophyllum daigremontianum.*

Cotyledon undulata

Habitat: South Africa.
Growth: Trunked succulent with thick, white-bloomed leaves with wavy edges. Large clusters of orange-yellow tubular flowers in spring and summer.
Use: Best in a sunny window.
Soil: Soilless mixture.
Feeding: 2 grams per litre ($\frac{1}{2}$ oz. per gallon) of water every 4 weeks (April–July).
Water: Summer, normal, but not too often. Winter, dry.
Light: Sunlight.
Heat: Summer, normal room temperature; winter, best at minimum 12° C. (55° F.).
Air: Dry air.
Re-potting: By cuttings of tip growths. Should be replaced from time to time, since old plants lose their bottom leaves.

Crassula portulacea (89)

Jade Plant

Habitat: South Africa.
Growth: Small tree-like succulent with a thick trunk and numerous branches. Thick, roundish leaves. White starry flowers in great profusion early in spring.

Use: Best in a window facing south.
Soil: Soilless mixture.
Feeding: 3 grams of fertiliser per litre (1 oz. per gallon) of water every 4 weeks (April–July).
Water: Summer, only when the plant is beginning to dry up completely. Winter, dry.
Light: Sunlight.
Heat: Normal temperature; winter, minimum 8° C. (45° F.).
Air: Dry air.
Re-potting: Seldom necessary.
Propagation: By cuttings in the spring.
Other species: See below.

Crassula falcata (90)

Growth: The thick, felted leaves are twisted and opposite, looking like ship's propellers. Deep red flowers in the early spring, in large, long-lasting inflorescences which grow so heavy that they have to be supported.
Use and culture: As for *Crassula portulacea.*

Crassula lactea

Growth: Small succulent with thick, blue-bloomed leaves. Small white starry flowers in an open inflorescence.
Use and culture: As for *Crassula portulacea.*

Crassula lycopodioides

Growth: Flimsy plant with thin upright shoots, the scaled leaves arranged in a

Crassula lycopodioides

regular pattern like the links in a zip fastener. White flowers.

Use and culture: As for *Crassula portulacea.*

Echeveria gibbiflora metallica (91)

Habitat: Mexico.

Growth: Large rosette of pretty, thick leaves with a metallic bronze sheen. The flowers are orange-red in spiked inflorescences. Long flowering period in the early spring.

Use: Best in windows facing south in full sunlight.

Culture: As for *Cotyledon undulata.*

Other species: See below.

Echeveria elegans (92)

Growth: Blue-bloomed rosette. Yellowy-white flowers in small clusters.

Use and culture: As for *Echeveria gibbiflora metallica.* Previously used for carpet bedding in gardens.

Kalanchoe blossfeldiana (93)

Habitat: Madagascar.

Growth: Compact plant with long-lasting, bright red flowers in thick tufts. The flowers on the dwarf varieties close up in the evening, while those of the taller varieties remain open day and night. Short-day plant which can be made to flower all year round by keeping in darkness for 14 hours out of 24 for 4 weeks.

Use: Attractive and very long-flowering ornamental plant.

Soil: Soilless mixture.

Feeding: 3 grams of fertiliser per litre (1 oz. per gallon) of water every 2 weeks (May–August).

Water: Summer, normal watering; more sparing in autumn and winter.

Light: Light or half-shade. The flowers are brightest in full sunlight.

Heat: Summer, normal temperature; winter, not below minimum 15°C. (60°F.).

Air: Will stand dry air.

Re-potting: After flowering has ceased, in pots which are not too large.

Cutting: Remove tops which have ceased to flower, for the sake of the continued development of the plant.

Propagation: By cuttings or seed.

Rochea coccinea

Habitat: South Africa, where the plant is protected.

Growth: Upright stems, with dense leaves arranged opposite one another and an umbel of crimson star flowers.

Use: Long-lasting, decorative sun plant with a powerful colour effect.

Soil: Soilless mixture.

Feeding: 3 grams of fertiliser per litre (1 oz. per gallon) of water every 2 weeks (March–July).

Water: Summer, normal; winter, dry.

Light: Sunlight.

Heat: Normal indoor temperature; winter, minimum 8°C. (45°F.).

Air: Dry air.

Re-potting: February, in pots which are not too large.

Cutting: Cut back to 15 cm. (6 in.) above the ground after flowering has ceased in June.

Propagation: By cuttings of side growths or by seed.

Rochea coccinea

Diseases: Spots on leaves if too damp during the winter.

Saxifragaceae

Hydrangea macrophylla

Habitat: Japan.
Growth: Vigorous bush, with brownish branches, inverted oval leaves and large, ball-shaped inflorescences, bearing coloured well-developed sepals and otherwise sterile flowers.
Use: Ornamental plant for large-scale arrangement in a conservatory. With light covering, can be left to winter out of doors in a warm growth location.
Soil: Soilless mixture or acid soil, pH 5·5.
Feeding: 5 grams of fertiliser per litre (1½ oz. per gallon) of water every week, from 6 weeks after re-potting until the beginning of August.
Water: Heavy consumption. Water twice on hot days. More sparingly in autumn and winter.
Light: No direct sunlight during flowering. Otherwise, a light growth spot.
Heat: Frost-free winter, possibly in a cellar; after that, normal indoor temperature.
Air: Humid air with spraying during and after flowering.
Re-potting: After flowering has ceased, re-pot in spacious pots and at the same time trim back the shoots which have been in bloom. The newly developed shoots will flower the following year.
Propagation: By cuttings in March.
Pests: Greenfly, thrips.
Forcing: Put in for forcing in January at minimum 15°C. (60°F.). Flowering will occur March–April at minimum 18°C. (65°F.). Remember to water generously, keep gently shaded and spray. After flowering has ceased in May, cut away the shoots which have been in bloom. Growth period is June–July, with plenty of nourishment and water. Resting period is August–

Hydrangea macrophylla

September, with moderate watering; light and cool growth location, but protect from frost.

Saxifraga stolonifera (94)

Mother of Thousands

Habitat: China and Japan.
Growth: Hanging plant with round, light-veined leaves having red undersides, gathered into rosettes. A 'beard' of red, wiry runners with new, small rosettes hangs down. White or light red flowers in upright inflorescences, May–August.
Use: Attractive, undemanding hanging-bowl plant.
Soil: Soilless mixture with good drainage.
Feeding: 3 grams of fertiliser per litre (1 oz. per gallon) of water every 2 weeks (March–September).
Water: Evenly moist from March until flowering has ceased in September. After that, keep quite dry.
Light: Very light spot near a window, otherwise the red leaves become discoloured.
Heat: Summer, normal temperature; winter, minimum 12–15°C. (55–60°F.).
Air: Dry indoor air.
Re-potting: Early spring in pots which are not too large but with good drainage.

Tolmiea menziesii

Propagation: By taking plantlets from the ends of the runners.
Pests: Greenfly.

Tolmiea menziesii

Pick-a-back plant

Habitat: North America.
Growth: Luxuriant green plant with downy leaves on stems. New plantlets are formed at the base of the leaves. By putting a leaf into water or planting it in damp sand, roots develop rapidly on the tiny plant. Runners with miniature plants striking roots are also formed.
Use: Very easily satisfied plant even in unfavourable conditions in dense shade. May be used as a hanging-bowl plant with the runners hanging down. Can be left to winter out of doors in mild winters, like a good virtually evergreen ground plant in the shade of other plants.
Soil: Soilless mixture, pH 7.
Feeding: 2 grams of fertiliser per litre ($\frac{1}{2}$ oz. per gallon) of water every week in the light season.
Water: Plenty; must never be allowed to dry out completely.
Light: Can manage with very little light, e.g. in shaded windows facing north, halls or stairways.
Heat: Normal room temperature. Will stand temperatures near freezing point.
Air: Dry indoor air.

Re-potting: Spring, when the roots have filled the pot.
Propagation: By leaf cuttings, which develop small plants at their base the whole year round, or by division of older plants in the spring.
Pests: Earwigs.
Variant: minima, which has small leaves, and is very profuse in its production of plantlets.

Pittosporaceae

Pittosporum tobira (95)

Habitat: China and Japan.
Growth: Evergreen bush with rhododendron-like leaves which are broadest towards the tip. Dense umbels of white flowers have an orange-blossom fragrance.
Use: Tub plant for conservatories, terraces or patios. Cool winter in a frost-free cold greenhouse or conservatory.
Soil: Nourishing garden soil with basic fertiliser added in the form of bonemeal (Animix) and Peraform.
Feeding: 5 grams of fertiliser per litre ($1\frac{1}{2}$ oz. per gallon) of water every week during the growth period.
Water: Summer, plenty; winter, just enough to prevent the soil ball from drying out completely.
Light: Slight shade. Light winter.
Heat: Summer, normal temperature; winter, minimum 5° C. (40° F.).
Air: Spraying in the spring.
Re-potting: Only occasionally.
Propagation: By seeding or cuttings.
Pests: Greenfly, scale insects.
Other species: See below.

Pittosporum undulatum

Growth: Dark, shiny leaves with slightly wavy edge. Somewhat reminiscent of the leaves of the coffee tree.
Use and culture: As for *Pittosporum tobira*.

Eriobotria japonica

Rosaceae

Eriobotria japonica

Loquat

Habitat: China and Japan.

Growth: Vigorous bush with 25-cm. (10-in.)-long, elliptical leaves; these have attractive patterns on the upper side, a brown felted appearance on the underside. The flat, fragrant flowers are gathered into large clusters. Large plum-like, yellow fruit with a delicate taste.

Use: Tub plant for large-scale arrangements, for example a cool conservatory or veranda. Summer, out of doors in a warm spot.

Soil: Nourishing garden soil with bonemeal added. Good drainage.

Feeding: 5 grams of fertiliser per litre (1½ oz. per gallon) of water every week during the growth period.

Water: Summer, plenty; winter, dry.

Light: Full sunlight.

Heat: Summer, warm; winter, minimum 5°C. (40° F.).

Air: Spray in spring.

Re-potting: Occasionally in deep tubs.

Propagation: By seed.

Pests: Greenfly, scale insects.

Rosa hybrids (96)

Growth: Densely branching, thorny bush with shiny, pinnate leaves and double flowers in many colours with and without fragrance.

Use: Ornamental plant, which is forced into flowering in winter or spring. Resting period in autumn in a cool spot. The types with dwarf-like growth and small flowers are to be preferred as indoor roses.

Soil: Soilless mixture or garden soil, with a high content of clay and sand, pH 6·5.

Feeding: 3 grams of fertiliser per litre of water (1 oz. per gallon) every week (February–August).

Water: Summer, normal watering; winter, moderate quantities, but do not allow the soil to dry out completely.

Light: Light and sunny position, possibly out of doors.

Heat: Autumn and winter, cool (minimum 5°C. (40° F.)). From January onwards, slowly rising to minimum 15°C. (60° F.).

Air: Damp air with spraying during forcing.

Re-potting: January, in deep pots. In the greenhouse the pots should be plunged in soil.

Cutting: Blooms which have finished flowering are cut away to leave 2 green leaves. Before commencement of forcing, cut out weak shoots and prune the remaining ones moderately.

Propagation: By cuttings in the spring, or by budding in the late summer.

Pests: Greenfly, rose beetle.

Diseases: Mildew, black spot.

Varieties: Miniature rose varieties. *Rosa chinensis minima*, which are 20–30 cm. (8–12 in.) tall, are to be preferred for indoor culture: 'Baby Masquerade' (light yellow/rose red), 'Colibri' (apricot-yellow/orange), 'Perle de Montserrat' (pale pink/pearl white) and 'Zwergkönig' (crimson).

NOTE: Forcing for several years in

succession may be difficult, which is why new plants should be potted. It is not advisable to move flowering plants.

Leguminosae

Cytisus canariensis (97)

Genista

Habitat: Canary Islands.
Growth: Silk-down-covered shoots, and finely divided leaves. Clusters of yellow 'pea flowers' from February to May.
Use: Ornamental plant in the spring.
Soil: Soilless mixture or loam with peat added, pH 6·5.
Feeding: 3 grams of fertiliser per litre (1 oz. per gallon) of water every week from January until flowering. After flowering has ceased, re-application should be done, then further application of fertiliser in the same doses until the end of August.
Water: From January to August, normal watering without drying out. Moderate watering after this.
Light: Likes full sunlight.
Heat: Summer, normal temperature, possibly out of doors. Autumn and winter, light and cool, but frost-free (minimum 5°C. (40°F.)) in December–January assists the development of buds). Subsequently, gradually warmer, up to 15°C. (60°F.) during flowering. If the plant is kept warmer than 15°C. (60°F.), flowering will not take place.
Air: Spray before and during flowering, otherwise dry air.
Re-potting: After flowering has ceased in deep, but not too spacious pots. Plant firmly, and avoid drying out.
Cutting: Plant may be shaped by stopping the summer shoots.
Propagation: By cuttings.
Other species: See below.

Cytisus × racemosus

Madeira Broom

Growth: Longer shoots with relatively dense down covering, and somewhat

earlier flowering than *Cytisus canariensis*. Use and cultivate otherwise in the same way. Has long-lasting, yellow flowers.

Acacia cyanophylla (98)

Habitat: Australia.
Growth: Elegant, thorny bush with entire 'leaves', which are expanded leaf stems—or phyllodes—in contrast with other *Acacia* species which have very finely divided, mimosa-like leaves. A profusion of yellow flowers in stemmed, round globe-like inflorescences.
Use: Good indoor plant for light, cool conditions. Best in windows facing east, west or north, or in light conservatories.
Soil: Soilless mixture, or light sandy loam with clay and compost mixed in.
Feeding: 2 grams of fertiliser per litre (½ oz. per gallon) of water every 2 weeks (April–July).
Water: The pot soil must always be moist, but must not be under water or be allowed to dry out completely. Good drainage is essential. Never have water in the base dish.
Light: Slight shade.
Heat: Summer, normal temperature, possibly outside in the sun and sheltered. Winter, minimum 8°C. (45°F.).
Air: Will stand dry indoor air. Spray in the spring.
Re-potting: At yearly intervals after flowering has ceased in May.
Propagation: By cuttings or seed.
Pests: Mealy bugs, scale insects.
NOTE: Take care to water properly.
Other species: See below.

Acacia dealbata decurrens (99)

Mimosa

Growth: Finely divided leaves. Globe-shaped, yellow flowers are delightfully fragrant, almost like foam rubber in appearance.
Use: Imported early in spring as cut flowering branches from the Riviera,

which are sold under the name of Mimosa. Not suitable for indoor culture except in large conservatories.

Albizzia lophantha

Habitat: Australia.
Growth: First-year plants have a single main stem, older plants are frequently more ramified. The leaves are bipannate, and very decorative. The flowers grow from pale yellow, cylindrical inflorescences.
Use: Best in cool rooms or conservatories. Summer, out of doors on a balcony or terrace. One-year plants are best for indoor culture.
Soil: Soilless mixture.
Feeding: 2 grams of fertiliser per litre ($\frac{1}{3}$ oz. per gallon) of water every 2 weeks (April–August).
Water: Evenly damp. Never allow to dry out completely, or to stand in water.
Light: Sunlight.
Heat: Summer, normal temperature; winter, minimum 2° C. (36° F.).
Air: Damp, not enclosed.
Re-potting: By seeds, which are sown at a high temperature in January.

Erythrina crista-galli

Lobster-claw

Habitat: Brazil.
Growth: Sub-shrub with 3-fingered leaves and colourful, coral red flowers on 60-cm. (24-in.)-long inflorescences. Flowering period, August–September.
Use: Tub plant for conservatories or large windows facing south. Summer, on a terrace or in a flower room.
Soil: Soilless mixture.
Feeding: 3 grams of fertiliser per litre (1 oz. per gallon) of water every 2 weeks (April–August).
Water: Summer, plenty. Never allow to dry out. Completely dry in winter.
Light: Full light and sunny spot.

Lotus berthelotii

Heat: Summer, normal temperature. From October to April, best at minimum 5° C. (40° F.).
Air: Summer, fresh air; winter, completely dry.
Re-potting: April.
Propagation: By seed; should be sown with bottom heat in January.

Lotus berthelotii

Habitat: Teneriffe.
Growth: Herbaceous perennial with creeping and hanging stems covered with silver down, and finely divided leaves. The large scarlet flowers, shaped like a bird's beak, appear in the early spring.
Use: Hanging-basket plant for a sunny window or conservatory. Winter, resting period, during which the top withers away.
Soil: Soilless mixture.
Feeding: 2 grams of fertiliser per litre ($\frac{1}{2}$ oz. per gallon) of water every week during the growth period.

Water: Spring and summer, plenty of water. When drying out, all leaves are shed. Winter, fairly dry.
Light: Sunny growth spot.
Heat: Normal room temperature, but very cool though absolutely frost-free in winter.
Air: Spraying.
Re-potting: August.
Propagation: By seed or cuttings of young shoots in spring.

Mimosa pudica

Sensitive Plant

Habitat: Brazil.
Growth: Branching bush with feather-cut, sensitive leaves which fold up or hang down limply when touched, in strong winds or when exposed to sharp fluctuations in temperature. When the stimulus is withdrawn, the leaves and stems become distended with sap once more. When in darkness the leaves fold up in a sleeping position and do not react to being touched. The small, red-dish-mauve flowers are gathered into a globe-shaped inflorescence.
Use: Interesting but not particularly durable indoor plant. Rejuvenation of half-withered plants by cutting back is not possible, therefore it must be cultivated as an annual.
Soil: Soilless mixture.
Feeding: 2 grams of fertiliser per litre ($\frac{1}{2}$ oz. per gallon) of water every 2 weeks (April–August).
Water: Normal watering the whole year round. In spring and summer, the soil must not dry out between waterings.
Light: Half-shade or sunshine.
Heat: In growth period, over minimum 18° C. (65° F.); in winter, somewhat cooler (minimum 15° C. (60° F.)).
Air: Very damp air in spring and summer, otherwise normal indoor air.
Re-potting: February. Older, unattractive plants should be discarded in favour of new 1-year plants.
Cutting back: Small plants can be stopped at the 4th or 6th leaf, in order to produce better branching.
Propagation: By seeds, which can be sown several at a time to each pot, over minimum 15° C. (60° F.) in February–March.

Onagraceae

Fuchsia hybrida (100)

Habitat: Tropical America.
Growth: Small, deciduous bush with hanging, lantern-like flowers in many colour combinations, especially white, pink, mauve, red and violet. There are also double varieties.
Use: Easy indoor plant in light, but not too warm, windows or conservatories. Summer, on a balcony or terrace. Older specimens can be cultivated as bushes or standard tub plants.
Soil: Soilless mixture.
Feeding: 3 grams of fertiliser per litre (1 oz. per gallon) of water every week

Mimosa pudica

(March–September). Flowering will be meagre if insufficient nourishment is given.
Water: Evenly damp soil; must not dry out completely. Winter, very dry.
Light: Half shade. Winter, light.
Heat: Normal temperature in summer; winter, best at minimum 10° C. (50° F.).
Air: Damp air, with frequent spraying.
Re-potting: February.
Cutting: Cut back branches on re-potting in the spring. Trunked plants are formed by tying up a single growth to a bamboo cane. All side shoots from the ground and up along the trunk should be removed, and the main stem stopped at its full height, from which the branches will radiate.
Propagation: By cuttings in the spring.
Pests: Greenfly.
Varieties: Very many varieties, among which some are suitable for hanging-bowls, some for balcony-boxes and some for use as pot plants.
NOTE: Very dry and cool winter. Remember to remove withered leaves so that nourishment is not used for fruit bearing. The fruit is, however, edible.

Punicaceae

Punica granatum (101)

Pomegranate

Habitat: Mediterranean region.
Growth: Up to 2 m. (6 ft.) in height. Light green bush with small, shiny leaves positioned in pairs on red stems. The sturdy, garnet-red flowers grow 3 by 3 on strong dwarf-shoots. Varieties are to be found with white, yellow, pale pink and 2-colour-striped flowers; there are also double forms. The dwarf-form, which is normally used in indoor culture, flowers from its second year of life, but the main type does not flower until later. The fruit seldom ripens in a British summer.
Use: The main type is used as a tub plant in a conservatory and, in summer, on a warm terrace or in an outside room. The dwarf form is a rewarding indoor plant.
Soil: Soilless mixture.
Feeding: 3 grams per litre of water (1 oz. per gallon) every 2 weeks (March–August).
Water: Plenty during summer, without allowing constant dampness; drier from March to October.
Light: Full sunlight.
Heat: Normal temperature in summer in an airy window, or possibly out of doors. Winter, minimum 8° C. (45° F.).
Air: Spray during the spring and summer, otherwise dry air.
Re-potting: February.
Cutting: Nip small shoots when re-potting; this produces a better crown form.
Propagation: By cuttings over high bottom heat.
Variant: P.g. 'nana', 50 cm. (20 in.) high. This dwarf form is better suited to indoor culture than the main type. Otherwise the same cultivation requirements.

Myrtaceae

Eucalyptus globulus (102)

Blue Gum

Habitat: Australia.
Growth: Rapid-growing, evergreen tree with angular trunks or stems. On young plants, the aromatic, oval, blue-bloomed leaves are non-petiolate—unstalked—and opposite. Later, the narrow petiolate, half-moon-shaped, hanging adult leaves appear. Planted in Southern Europe as a means of drying up malaria swamps, as the tree absorbs and evaporates large quantities of water.
Use: Young plants are ornamental indoor plants. They quickly become too big for ordinary windows, however. Older plants are therefore best used in halls, conservatories or on verandas.

Soil: Soilless mixture.

Feeding: Large appetite. 3 grams per litre (1 oz. per gallon) of water every week (February–October).

Water: A lot of water during growth period, with no drying out in between. When kept cool for the winter, give enough water to prevent the soil from drying out altogether.

Light: As much as possible. The blue colour of the leaves will fade if the plant is put in too shady a spot.

Heat: Summer, normal temperature; winter, minimum 8° C. (45° F.).

Air: Will stand dry, indoor air, as long as sufficient water is given.

Re-potting: Young plants are re-potted every year in February, older plants somewhat less frequently.

Cutting: Bushy plants are formed by nipping the top shoots at the right time.

Propagation: By seed.

Myrtus communis

Myrtle

Habitat: Mediterranean countries.

Growth: Evergreen bush, the branches of which are often used for bridal crowns or bouquets. The small, coriaceous, dark green leaves have an aro-

Dizygotheca elegantissima

matic fragrance and flavour. The flowers are snow-white, positioned on short stems in the axils. Flowering period, June–September.

Use: Undemanding indoor plant for windows facing east or west.

Soil: Soilless mixture, with good drainage.

Feeding: 4 grams per litre (1¼ oz. per gallon) of water, every week (March–July).

Water: Carefully with rainwater or some other calcium-free water. Both constant dampness and complete drying out should be avoided.

Light: Light location away from direct sunlight. The plant should be turned frequently, so that it can develop evenly on all sides.

Heat: Normal room temperature; winter, minimum 8° C. (45° F.).

Air: Dry room air.

Re-potting: February, in pots which are not too large.

Cutting: The plant can be shaped by pruning and stopping young shoots; it can be grown as a standard with a globe-shaped crown. Flowering is reduced if cut back too extensively.

Myrtus communis

Propagation: By grafting in early spring.
Pests: Scale insects.

Araliaceae

Dizygotheca elegantissima

Spider Plant

Habitat: New Caledonia.
Growth: Elegant leaf plant, 50 cm. (20 in.) high. Narrow, fingered, reddish-brown leaves with jagged edges. Older plants have larger leaves and small greenish flowers. The flowering form goes under the name *Dizygotheca kerchoveana.*
Use: Best in a window facing east or west, or a warm conservatory. Lasts for many years indoors.
Soil: Soilless mixture.
Feeding: 3 grams per litre (1 oz. per gallon) of water every two weeks (March–September). Never give nourishment to dry soil balls.
Water: Summer, normal watering; winter, more moderate.
Light: Half shade; never direct sunlight.
Heat: Normal room temperature. Winter, not below minimum 15°C. (60°F.). Requires more heat than other members of the *Araliaceae.*
Air: Needs damp air with frequent spraying.
Re-potting: Every 2 or 3 years in February.
Propagation: By seed.
Pests: Red spider mites.
NOTE: Needs absolutely damp air. Young plants are difficult to acclimatise, but older established plants may thrive for many years in the same spot.

Fatshedera lizei   (103)

Growth: A cross between *Fatsia japonica moseri*, the Castor Oil tree, and *Hedera helix hibernica*, Irish Ivy. Vigorous, half-climbing plant with 5-lobed, dark green leaves.

Use: Leaf plant for halls, conservatories and large windows. Rapidly grows too large for normal windows, but can be cut back and thus adjusted to the space available. Will stand an indoor atmosphere better than many *Araliaceae.*
Culture: As for *Dizygotheca elegantissima*, but will stand wintering at a cooler temperature (minimum 10°C. (50°F.)).
Cutting: To compensate for the plant's naturally poor branching, cutting back each year in February can be recommended.
Pests: Scale insects, red spider mites.

Fatsia japonica

Castor Oil Tree

Habitat: Japan.
Growth: Vigorous foliage plant with 5–7-lobed leaves.
Use: Will last for many years at normal room temperature, or in a cool conservatory.
Culture: As for *Dizygotheca elegantissima*, but requires a lower temperature in winter (minimum 10°C. (50°F.)).
Cutting: Cutting back in February will give a better spread of branches.
Pests: Greenfly, scale insects, red spider mites.
Variant: moseri.
NOTE: If a choice has to be made between the 3 Aralia types, remember that *Fatshedera* is the easiest one to handle, while *Dizygotheca* is the most ornamental.

Hedera canariensis   (104)

Canary Island Ivy

Habitat: Canary Islands.
Growth: Climbing plant with suction roots on its stems and large almost undivided leaves.
Use: Trellis plant in shaded windows, on

Hedera canariensis 'Variegata'

a wall, and as decoration for large rooms such as halls and vestibules. May also be used as a hanging-bowl plant, in rooms and conservatories.

Soil: Soilless mixture.

Feeding: 3 grams per litre (1 oz. per gallon) of water every week (April–September).

Water: Normal, but do not allow to dry out. Water more sparingly in the winter, however.

Light: Full or half-shade. At high room temperatures in the winter, give somewhat more light.

Heat: Does well in cool rooms.

Air: As humid as possible.

Re-potting: February, in pots which are not too large.

Cutting: Stopping young shoots may induce branching.

Tying up: The dwarf varieties are best used as hanging plants without tying up. Other types should be tied to wire or bamboo trellises. Sucks firmly on to quite smooth wall surfaces, from which the stems may later be difficult to remove.

Propagation: By grafting top shoots in August.

Pests: Scale insects, red spider mites.

Variants: 'Foliis variegatis' with ivory-blotched leaves.

Other species: See below.

Hedera helix (105)

Ivy

Habitat: Europe.

Growth: Well-known garden plant, which also thrives indoors, even in poor growth conditions.

Use and culture: As for *Hedera canariensis.*

Variants: A few of the many are: *cavendishii,* with irregular, white leaf patterns; *crispa,* with small, frizzy leaves; *hibernica,* Irish ivy, which has very small leaves with fine, light net-patterns; *ovata,* with almost heart-shaped leaves; 'Pittsburgh', Star ivy, which has a very dense and compact growth, with short runners sending out shoots from all axils, which is suitable for smaller windows; and *sagittaefolia,* Arrow-leaf ivy, with deeply indented, almost arrow-shaped leaves.

Ericaceae

Erica gracilis (106)

Christmas Heather

Habitat: South Africa.

Growth: Well-branched little bush, with tiny, fresh-green leaves and small, bell-shaped flowers in white, pink and purple. Flowers in late autumn and mid-winter.

Use: Long-lasting indoor flower in cool conditions. In Germany it is used as a seasonal plant for All Hallows Day, the 1st November.

Soil: Peat, sand or garden soil with no calcium content, pH 4.

Feeding: If the plant is in soil with as low a nutrition content as peat, some fertiliser must be given, but the plant will not stand a high concentration of salt in the soil, as this will scorch the roots. So water carefully with 1 gram of ordinary indoor plant fertiliser per litre ($\frac{1}{4}$ oz. per gallon) every 2 weeks, alternating with 1 gram of urea per litre

Hedera helix sagittaefolia

($\frac{1}{4}$ oz. per gallon), but only in May and June.

Water: Plenty. If allowed to dry out even once, the plant may shed its leaves and wither. Remember also to keep the soil moist in winter.

Light: As well-lit a situation as possible. *Erica* species are typical sun plants.

Heat: Should spend the summer out of doors. Winter, minimum 10° C. (50° F.).

Air: Spring and summer, humid air, with spraying. Drier in winter.

Re-potting: After flowering has ceased in the early spring, in pots which are not too large. Water thoroughly before re-potting.

Cutting: Young shoots should be nipped in the early spring, so as to produce bushy plants. Nipping after 1st May produces poorer flowering.

Propagation: By cuttings in the spring.

NOTE: The plant should be kept in a light and cool—but frost-free—spot after flowering has ceased.

Other species: See below.

Erica hiemalis

Habitat: South Africa.
Growth: Larger and more open than *Erica gracilis*. Flowers in February–March, with long, tube-like flowers in pale pink shades.
Use and culture: As above, but will not stand such extensive nipping, and not after 1st June.

Erica ventricosa

Habitat: South Africa.
Growth: Vigorous, dense growth with large, urn-shaped, light red or purple-red flowers gathered together at the end of the stems. Flowering period, May–July. Longer flowering if in a cool place.
Use and culture: As for *Erica gracilis*.

Erica wilmorei

Habitat: South Africa.
Growth: Upright growth, with very large, long tube-like flowers in shades of red. Flowering period, April–May.
Use and culture: As for *Erica gracilis*.

Rhododendron simsii   (107)

Indian Azalea

Habitat: Eastern Asia.
Growth: Small evergreen bush covered with brown down. The coriaceous leaves are dark green with lighter undersides, the flowers are both single and double, in white and all shades of red. Natural flowering in May, but now forced in nurseries commercially for sale from August to May.

Use: Colourful ornamental plant for autumn, winter and spring. Repeated flowering may present some difficulty with older plants under indoor culture.

Soil: Soilless mixture, or a special 'azalea soil' consisting of a mixture of peat, spruce or pine needles together with well-rotted horse manure. pH 4–4.5.

Feeding: 3 grams per litre (1 oz. per gallon) of water every week (March–August).

Water: Only use rainwater or some other soft water, possibly mains water neutralised by 1 gram ammonium sulphate per litre ($\frac{1}{4}$ oz. per gallon). Water generously during flowering and growth, from the top and not into base dishes. Once a week the plant should be bathed by dipping the entire pot into lukewarm water, so that the soil ball is thoroughly wetted. If allowed to dry out even once, the plant is liable to shed its leaves and possibly wither away completely. During the development of buds in the early autumn, water generously.

Light: Full or half-shade. Flowering may cease too quickly in full sunlight.

Heat: Flowering lasts longer in a cool place. After flowering has ceased, the plant should be placed in a warm spot away from direct sunlight out of doors. In September it should be taken back indoors and placed in a light, cool spot (minimum 10°C. (50°F.)), until forcing begins in December.

Air: Damp air with spraying during the growth period.

Re-potting: Directly after flowering has ceased in May–June. Make sure the soil ball is thoroughly wet before re-potting.

Propagation: By cuttings or by grafting.

Diseases: Leaf shedding as a result of drought. Yellow leaves and shoot tips in soil containing calcium.

NOTE: Winter and spring: Flowering period with plenty of water, a lot of nourishment and a temperature of 15°C. (60°F.). Re-pot in May. May–August: Growth period with plenty of water, a lot of nourishment and a warm spot out of doors. September: Resting period and formation of buds, with moderate watering, no nourishment and a cool location (minimum 10°C. (50°F.)). Forcing, January–March.

Varieties: A large number of varieties in many colours and shapes.

Other species: See below.

Rhododendron obtusum

Growth: Not such compact growth as *Rhododendron simsii*, and smaller,

elegant flowers. Use and culture otherwise the same.

Primulaceae

Cyclamen persicum giganteum (108)

Cyclamen

Habitat: Middle East.

Growth: Tuberous plant with wide petiolate, heart-shaped leaves which have attractive patterns. The flowers are lifted up over the foliage by succulent, smooth stems, and the petals, which are attractively swept back, may be found in white and all shades of red. There are also types with semi-double flowers, and others with fringed petals. A good commercial plant should have vigorous foliage with firm stems, upright flower stems and a large number of buds on the way up from the tuber.

Use: Outstanding and long-lasting ornamental plant which is in season in autumn, winter and spring.

Soil: Soilless mixture with good drainage.

Feeding: 3 grams of fertiliser per litre (1 oz. per gallon) of water every week in summer, every 2 weeks in winter, and always to a soil ball which is already moist.

Water: Plenty in summer; winter, as required, without allowing to dry out. The tuber itself and the flower buds on it must not be wetted. Watering in a base dish is recommended. Superfluous water which has not been absorbed after half an hour should be poured away.

Light: Full or half-shade. Light in winter, but without direct sunlight.

Heat: November–February, minimum 10°C. (50°F.); the rest of the year, minimum 15–18°C. (60–65°F.). In warm rooms, incipient buds will not develop and existing flowers will fade quickly.

Air: Spray frequently in summer. In the six months of the winter season, from October, the air should be kept dry.

Re-potting: After flowering has ceased in April–May. At the same time, remove old dry roots.

Propagation: By seed.

Pests: Greenfly, thrips.

NOTE: The plant should be maintained in growth the whole year round without a resting period. Cool and light in winter, cool and damp in summer. The soil ball should never be allowed to dry out completely. New leaves should develop before the old ones wither away.

Primula malacoides (109)

Fairy Primrose

Habitat: Yunnan province in China.

Growth: Annual herbaceous plant with a rosette of long-stemmed oval leaves, and many whorls of small, stalked flowers in white, pink, mauve or red. The whole plant is more or less white-powdered.

Use: Ornamental plant in winter and spring. Can seldom be forced a second time.

Soil: Peat, with sandy soil and compost mixed in, possibly loamless compost. Good drainage.

Feeding: 1 gram of fertiliser per litre ($\frac{1}{4}$ oz. per gallon) of water every 2 weeks. The roots are scorched if there is too high a content of fertiliser salts in the soil.

Water: The soil ball must always be moist, but never water in the base dish. Dried out plants can be rescued by immersing the pot in a container with lukewarm water for a couple of hours.

Light: Half-shade, never direct sun. The colour of the flowers will fade, however, if too little light is given.

Heat: Cool location. Winter, not more than minimum 10° C. (50° F.).

Air: Humid air.

Re-potting: The plant is usually discarded after flowering has ceased.

Cutting: Stems which have finished flowering are removed, to encourage

Primula obconica

new flower stems to form and extend the flowering period 3–4 months.

Propagation: By seed.

Other species: See below.

Primula obconica

Habitat: China.

Growth: Vigorous, perennial indoor primula, with long-stemmed, roundish, whole-edged leaves, and long flower stems bearing large balls of flat-collared flowers in white, pink, red and violet. Both leaves and stems are covered with gland hairs; these contain a substance which may cause dermatitis in susceptible people, and anyone allergic to this should wear gloves when handling the plants. In Germany, varieties containing practically no irritant are produced under the name *Nonprimina Bayernblut*.

Use: Rewarding ornamental plant for winter and spring.

Culture: As for *Primula malacoides*. But since the plant is a perennial, it must be re-potted after flowering has ceased in May, in pots which are not too large. The soil should be more sandy than the

Primula sinensis

mixture specified for the above type. After re-potting, the plant should be placed in a damp, semi-shaded location for the whole of the summer. Has no particular resting period.

Primula sinensis

Habitat: China.
Growth: Long-stemmed, segmented, downy leaves. Dense inflorescence, with large, flat-collared flowers on relatively short stems. Flower colours can be white, pink, red, blue and violet.
Use: Good indoor plant for cool, light windows.
Culture: As for *Primula obconica*. Re-potting after flowering has ceased. Sensitive to lingering moisture, which is why the pot must have good drainage. The root neck should be placed above the surface of the soil when re-potting, so that the plant almost rests upon the ground, supported by a couple of matches or small sticks. Planting too deeply will cause rot in the neck of the plant.

Primula kewensis (110)

Growth: A cross between the Primula species *floribunda* and *verticillata*

produced at Kew Gardens, in England. Has longish, powdery leaves. A tall stem with whorls of short-stalked butter-yellow flowers; indeed, the only indoor primula with yellow blossom.
Use: Annual ornamental plant for cool, light windows.
Culture: As for *Primula malacoides*. Difficult to cultivate for more than one season.

Plumbaginaceae

Plumbago capensis (111)

Plumbago

Habitat: South Africa.
Growth: Long, pendulous stems with light green leaves, arranged spirally. The light blue, phlox-like flowers are borne in large umbels, and the unusually long flowering period extends from March to November.
Use: Long-flowering indoor plant for light windows. Older plants require supporting or tying-up. Large plants in tubs can be left out of doors for the summer.
Soil: Soilless mixture.
Feeding: 3 grams of fertiliser per litre (1 oz. per gallon) of water every week (March–November).
Water: Plenty. Drier from November to February.
Light: As light as possible in south-facing window. The pot should be protected against drying out in direct sunshine.
Heat: Most luxuriant flowering at high temperatures. From November to February, best at minimum 12°C. (55°F.). Must not be placed in a cellar. The roots should always be kept cool.
Air: Dry indoor air.
Re-potting: February.
Cutting: Prune long shoots at the same time as re-potting.
Propagation: By cuttings.

232

Polemoniaceae

Cobaea scandens (112)

Habitat: Mexico.
Growth: Rapidly-growing, perennial climbing plant, the tendrils of which support the stems together. Bell-shaped, violet flowers appear throughout the summer and autumn.
Use: Normally treated as an annual climbing plant for use indoors or out of doors on a trellis. Will survive the winter easily if protected from frost, and can be used as a perennial indoor plant for trellising in large windows and cool conservatories. A permanent trellis is unsuitable where the plant cannot spend the winter in the growth location, but must be moved to a cooler spot.
Soil: Soilless mixture.
Feeding: 2 grams per litre ($\frac{1}{2}$ oz. per gallon) of water every week (March–September).
Water: Plenty in summer; winter, dry.
Light: Flowers best in a light location.
Heat: Summer, normal temperature; winter, minimum 8° C. (46° F.).
Air: Ordinary indoor air.
Re-potting: Early spring, before forcing begins at normal room temperature.
Cutting: Extensive pruning at the time of re-potting. In addition, thin out the trails a few times during the course of the summer in order to get air to the plant and to promote flowering.
Propagation: By seed.
Varieties: There is a white variant.

Convolvulaceae

Pharbitis tricolor (113)

Morning Glory

Habitat: Central America.
Growth: Vigorous, annual twining plant with a great profusion of large, heart-shaped leaves and red, violet or blue trumpet-shaped bindweed flowers, each of which only opens for a single day.
Use: Trellis plant for a large, bright window, conservatory or outdoor summer location free from wind.
Soil: Soilless mixture.
Feeding: 2 grams per litre ($\frac{1}{2}$ oz. per gallon) of water every week (April–September).
Water: Plenty.
Light: Sunlight.
Heat: Normal summer temperature.
Air: Spray during hot weather.
Re-potting: This is only an annual.
Tying-up: The stems must be spread out on the trellis at the start, so that they do not tangle.
Cutting: Removal of withered flowers assists further flowering.
Propagation: By seeding under glass in March.
Pests: Greenfly, red spider mites.
Varieties: 'Clark's Blue' (sky blue) and 'Scarlett O'Hara' (claret-coloured).

Boraginaceae

Heliotropium arborescens

Heliotrope

Habitat: Peru.
Growth: Evergreen sub-shrub with very dark green, veined leaves, and flat umbels of dark violet, delicately fragrant flowers in summer and autumn.

Heliotropium arborescens

Use: Ordinary plant for putting out in balcony-boxes, flower-bowls and garden-beds. Also suitable as a garden plant on the lines of *Geraniums* and *Busy Lizzie.*

Soil: Soilless mixture.

Feeding: 2 grams per litre ($\frac{1}{2}$ oz. per gallon) of water every week (May–August).

Water: Plenty.

Light: Bright window, but not exposed to scorching sunshine.

Heat: Summer, normal room temperature; winter, minimum 12°C. (55°F.).

Air: Spray frequently in hot weather.

Re-potting: Spring, before growth begins.

Cutting: Nip out the tops of the shoots in spring in order to shape the plant and to provide several flowering shoots.

Propagation: By cuttings in autumn and/or spring.

Solanaceae

Browallia speciosa

Habitat: Tropical America.

Growth: Sub-shrub, cultivated as an

Browallia speciosa

annual. The leaves are broad and lance-shaped. Blue, bell-shaped flowers, 4 cm. ($1\frac{3}{4}$ in.) across; only a few appear simultaneously, but the plant has a long flowering period.

Use: A non-permanent, undemanding indoor plant, which can be made to flower at almost any season of the year.

Soil: Soilless mixture.

Feeding: 2 grams per litre ($\frac{1}{2}$ oz. per gallon) of water every 2 weeks (March–August).

Water: Normal watering, but do not allow to dry out.

Light: Light or half-shade.

Heat: Normal, but not too high room temperature.

Air: Spray in hot weather.

Re-potting: Retention over the winter and re-potting are not worth while.

Cutting: Nip or cut back after main flowering period, as this will enable the plant to flower again.

Propagation: By seed.

Brunfelsia calycina (114)

Habitat: Brazil.

Growth: Small bush with coriaceous, dark green leaves. Large, flat-collared, violet flowers which, when flowering is coming to an end, fade to a weak shade of pale blue. Normal flowering period from February to September; under good growth conditions, the whole year round.

Use: Easy, long-flowering indoor plant.

Soil: Soilless mixture with good drainage.

Feeding: 3 grams per litre (1 oz. per gallon) of water every 2 weeks (March–September), but only apply to moist soil balls.

Water: Normal watering, but do not allow lingering moisture during the growth period. Sparingly during the winter, but do not allow to dry out completely.

Light: Half-shade; winter, light.

Heat: Normal room temperature, but

avoid major fluctuations. Winter, not below minimum 15° C. (60° F.).

Air: Damp air with frequent spraying.

Re-potting: February in flat pots.

Cutting: Nip the top shoots of young plants.

Propagation: By cuttings over minimum 30° C. (85° F.) bottom heat in spring.

Variants: eximea, with large, purple-violet flowers, and *floribunda,* which flowers most prolifically.

NOTE: In order to get air to the roots, loosen the top soil at suitable intervals or possibly top dress, but take care not to damage the roots at the surface of the soil.

Other species: See below.

Brunfelsia hopeana

Growth: Pale violet flowers in great profusion.

Use and culture: As for *Brunfelsia calycina,* but requires more heat. Sensitive to lingering moisture and drought. Best in a hothouse or heated conservatory.

Cestrum purpureum (115)

Habitat: Mexico.

Growth: Metre-high (3-ft.) bush with overhanging branches, large full-edged leaves and clusters of tubular purple flowers from March to July.

Use: Space-consuming, elegant plant for large flower windows or conservatories.

Soil: Soilless mixture.

Feeding: 2 grams per litre ($\frac{1}{2}$ oz. per gallon) of water every 2 weeks (March–August).

Water: Plenty during the summer, very dry in winter.

Light: Half-shade.

Heat: Normal temperature in summer; winter, minimum 12° C. (55° F.).

Air: Normal indoor air.

Re-potting: Early spring, before the growth period begins.

Cutting: Cut back when re-potting.

Propagation: By cuttings over high bottom heat.

Datura suaveolens (116)

Angel's Trumpet

Habitat: Mexico.

Growth: Sturdy bush with soft, slightly downy leaves and large white, trombone-like hanging flowers having their tips curved backwards. Delicate fragrance. Flowering period, June–November.

Use: Small plants for indoor use. Larger plants are more suitable for tubs in halls or conservatories, or on a sunny, sheltered terrace out of doors during the summer.

Soil: Soilless mixture.

Feeding: 5 grams per litre (1$\frac{1}{2}$ oz. per gallon) of water every week (February–September). Large appetite.

Water: Plenty. Drought causes the leaves to droop limply.

Light: Sunlight or half-shade. Light location during the winter.

Heat: Summer, normal temperature; winter, minimum 10° C. (50° F.).

Air: Will stand dry air. Avoid drops of water on flowers, or moisture dripping from trees out of doors in the summer.

Re-potting: February, in pots which are not too large, or in tubs.

Cutting: The crown can be shaped by light pruning in February. Standard trees are developed by the removal of side shoots on the stem up to the required height.

Propagation: By cuttings in early spring.

Pests: Red spider mites, snails and slugs.

NOTE: The sap and seeds are *poisonous.*

Other species: See below.

Datura sanguinea

Growth: 20 cm. (8 in.) long, red and yellowy-green funnel-shaped flowers in autumn.

Use and culture: As for *Datura suaveolens.* No definite resting period.

Solanum capsicastrum (117)
Christmas Cherry

Habitat: Southern Brazil.
Growth: Small bush with narrow, shiny, lance-shaped leaves and white flowers in May. Round or oval fruits in shades of orange and red develop in the late summer.
Use: Easily satisfied indoor plant, decorative when bearing fruit.
Soil: Soilless mixture.
Feeding: 3 grams per litre (1 oz. per gallon) of water every 2 weeks (April–August).
Water: Summer, plenty; winter, moderate. No real resting period.
Light: Semi-shaded or light location. Sunshine needed for the attractive fruit colouring.
Heat: Normal room temperature during the flowering and fruit-bearing periods. After the fruit have fallen in winter, cooler (minimum 15° C. (60° F.)).
Air: Dry room air.
Re-potting: Early spring, well before flowering commences, but the plant is usually treated as an annual and discarded after bearing fruit.
Propagation: By seed.
Pests: Greenfly, thrips, red spider mites.
Other species: See below.

Solanum pseudocapsicum

Habitat: Madeira.
Growth: Produces slightly larger berries than *Solanum capsicastrum.* Use and culture otherwise the same.

Scrophulariaceae
Calceolaria herbeohybrida (118)
Slipper Flower

Habitat: Andes Mountains.
Growth: One-year herbaceous plant

Solanum pseudocapsicum

with succulent, green leaves and brightly coloured, blown-out, spotted flowers with a mesh pattern.
Use: Ornamental plant, but only while flowering in the spring. Short-lived.
Soil: Soilless mixture.
Feeding: Unnecessary, if the plants are bought already in flower and thrown out after flowering has ceased.
Water: Plenty of water, and do not allow to dry out. May need watering several times a day in hot conditions.
Light: Light location away from direct sunshine.
Heat: As cool a spot as possible. The flowers last longest at minimum 10–12° C. (50–55° F.).
Air: Very damp air with frequent spraying.
Re-potting: The plant is thrown out after flowering has ceased.
Propagation: Seeding in July–August. Transplant one month later, and pot in small pots in October. Maintain a constant temperature of minimum 12° C. (55° F.), but in order to assist the development of flower buds, subject to a 'cool treatment' at minimum 8° C. (47° F.) for a month as soon as the plant has acquired 5–6 green leaves. After that, revert to minimum 12° C. (55° F.), also during the flowering period.
Pests: Slugs and snails.
Diseases: Grey mould.

Hebe andersonii

Habitat: New Zealand.
Growth: Small, evergreen bush with lance-shaped leaves and pale, violet-blue flowers in brush-like inflorescences, August–October.
Use: Chiefly an indoor foliage plant, but can also be used out of doors in the summer in balcony-boxes, tubs or in borders.
Soil: Soilless mixture.
Feeding: 3 grams per litre (1 oz. per gallon) of water every 2 weeks (April–August).
Water: Summer, normal watering; winter, very dry.
Light: Light and sunny location, especially in the winter.
Heat: Relatively cool. Winter, frost free, best at minimum 5° C. (40° F.).
Air: Dry indoor air.
Re-potting: February.
Propagation: By cuttings in spring.
Variant: 'Variegata', with white-edged, green leaves, which is the one most often cultivated.

Gesneriaceae

Achimenes coccinea

Habitat: Central America.
Growth: Cone-shaped stem tubers with

Hebe andersonii

upright, down-covered stems. The leaves are oval, serrated and down-covered; the plant has flat, plate-like, red flowers in the axils. Flowering period, June–October.
Use: Luxuriantly flowering indoor plant for windows facing east or west.
Soil: Soilless mixture.
Feeding: 3 grams per litre (1 oz. per gallon) of water every 2 weeks during growth period, until flowering commences.
Water: Keep the soil evenly moist from March to October. Always take the chill off the water, and avoid water dripping on to the leaves and flowers. Keep completely dry during the resting period, October–February.
Light: Half-shade.
Heat: Force in March–April at minimum 20–25° C. (70–80° F.). Afterwards, normal room temperature until October. Keep at minimum 10° C. (50° F.) during the winter.
Air: Slightly damp air during forcing in March–April, otherwise normal indoor air.
Re-potting: The tubers should be potted in February, 3–5 in each pot, covered with 2 cm. (1 in.) of soil. Further re-potting unnecessary.
Propagation: By division of tubers.
Pests: Greenfly.
NOTE: Keep to the October–February resting period with the temperature at a minimum 10° C. (50° F.) and completely dry.
Other species: See below.

Achimenes longiflora   (119)

Growth: Plain blue flowers. Also types in white, pink, scarlet and light and dark blue.
Use and culture: As for *Achimenes coccinea*.

Aeschynanthus lobbianus

Habitat: East Indies.
Growth: In nature, an epiphyte on tree

Aeschynanthus lobbianus

trunks. Hanging stems with thick, dark green leaves. The bright red flowers are mounted in a downy, tubular calyx with dark stripes.

Use: Can be used as a flowering plant in windows facing east or west, as a hanging plant, or as a ground plant in a conservatory.

Soil: Soilless mixture.

Feeding: 3 grams per litre (1 oz. per gallon) every 2 weeks (March–September).

Water: The plant is kept completely dry for the whole of May to allow the development of flower buds. Otherwise normal watering. Only use lukewarm water. Do not pour water directly on to leaves and flowers.

Light: Full or half-shade.

Heat: During the resting period in May, less than minimum 15°C. (60°F.), otherwise around minimum 20°C. (70°F.).

Air: Humid.

Re-potting: April.

Propagation: By cuttings of shoot tips

238

or by cuttings from stem pieces in early spring.

Pests: Greenfly, red spider mites, snails and slugs.

Hypocyrta radicans (120)

Clog plant

Habitat: Brazil.

Growth: Upright or semi-hanging stems with thick, shiny oval leaves. The orange-red flowers are tube-like, pressed together in front, with an orange-yellow rim. Flowers in spring and summer.

Use: Ornamental flowering plant in summer. Evergreen indoor plant outside the flowering season.

Soil: Soilless mixture.

Feeding: 3 grams per litre (1 oz. per gallon) of water every 2 weeks (March–September). Only give nourishment when the soil ball is moist.

Water: Regular watering, without allowing to dry out, but no lingering moisture. Winter, more sparingly. Only use tepid water.

Light: Shaded or semi-shaded location; winter, lighter.

Heat: Summer, normal room temperature. Winter, minimum 15°C. (60°F.), but only minimum 12°C. (55°F.) during the 6 weeks in December–January when the buds are developing.

Air: Humid air.

Re-potting: February, in flat dishes.

Propagation: By top cuttings, which will strike roots at minimum 25°C. (77°F.) bottom heat.

Diseases: Ring markings appear on leaves when the water used for watering is too cold.

Pests: Greenfly.

Columnea hybrida (121)

Habitat: Costa Rica.

Growth: Hanging plant with thin trails, up to a metre (3 ft.) in length, densely covered with small, opposite reddish leaves. The flowers are orange-red in colour, and appear in the axils. From time to time, attractive red berries also appear.

Use: Good hanging-bowl plant in warm conditions, e.g. a conservatory.

Soil: Soilless mixture.

Feeding: 2 grams per litre ($\frac{1}{2}$ oz. per gallon) of water, every week (January–September).

Water: Leave without water for the whole of December, the plant's resting period, in order to assist the formation of flower buds. After that, normal watering with tepid water, but without allowing to dry out, until September. More sparingly in October and November, gradually cutting down the amounts until the resting period. Additional flowering can be obtained by adding a month's extra rest at the height of the summer, with no water or nourishment and in a cool location.

Light: Half-shade, never direct sunlight.

Heat: During the resting period in December, minimum 10°C. (50°F.). After that, minimum 20°C. (70°F.) for the entire growth period until September. In autumn, minimum 15°C. (60°F.). Avoid major fluctuations in daytime temperature.

Air: High degree of air humidity. Keep the air damp, but do not spray directly on to the leaves, which will cause brown spots to appear.

Episcia reptans

Re-potting: In pans, after flowering has ceased.

Propagation: By cuttings from stems, which are covered with soil.

NOTE: Do not forget constant temperature, no draughts and humid air.

Varieties: 'Vega', with orange-red, yellow-throated flowers, and 'Capella'.

Other species: See below.

Columnea microphylla

Growth: Elegant hanging plant with thin stems and very small, green, downy leaves. Orange-red flowers have yellow throats and yellow stripes on their corolla tubes.

Use and culture: As for *Columnea hybrida*. Needs warmth.

Episcia reptans

Habitat: Columbia and Brazil.

Growth: Creeping stems with runners, which carry small plants. Downy, olive-green leaves with lighter veins and reddish undersides. Small, clear red flowers in the summer time.

Use: Good hanging-bowl plant in slightly shaded location.

Soil: Soilless mixture with good drainage.

Feeding: 2 grams per litre ($\frac{1}{2}$ oz. per gallon) of water every 2 weeks (April–August).

Water: Regular watering. Will not stand either drying out or too much water.

Light: Window facing east or west.

Heat: Not less than 15°C. (60°F.) during growth period, March–September. Winter, minimum 10°C. (50°F.).

Air: High degree of air humidity, but do not water or spray directly on to the foliage. Will not stand draughts.

Re-potting: April, in flat dishes.

Propagation: By runners which have taken root. Older plants are less attractive and should be replaced by new ones every 2 years.

Kohleria eriantha

Pests: Red spider mites, thrips, snails and slugs, wood lice.
NOTE: Needs warmth, damp air and very light location.

Kohleria eriantha

Habitat: Central America.
Growth: Scale-like tubers. Oval, dark green leaves with red down. Bell-shaped flowers with a narrow tube and collar inclined outwards. The flowers, which are thickly covered with down, are orange-red with yellow spots on their inner sides.
Use: Good indoor plant in a warm, shaded flower window.
Soil: Soilless mixture.
Feeding: 3 grams per litre (1 oz. per gallon) of water every 3 weeks (April–August).
Water: Even watering the whole year round, but must not dry out. Always use water at room temperature.
Light: Shaded or semi-shaded location.
Heat: Summer, minimum 25°C. (77°F.); winter, not less than 12°C. (55°F.).
Air: Damp air.
Re-potting: March, in flat pots.
Propagation: By division of tubers.
Pests: Thrips.

Rechsteineria cardinalis

Habitat: South America.
Growth: Tuberous plant with very soft, velvet-green leaves covered with fine down. Long, tube-like scarlet flowers. Flowering season, May–September.
Use: Best in warm, slightly shaded flower windows, or possibly conservatories.
Soil: Soilless mixture with good drainage.
Feeding: 2 grams per litre ($\frac{1}{2}$ oz. per gallon) of water every week from the beginning of growth to flowering. Only give nourishment to damp soil balls.
Water: Keep constantly damp in spring and summer. After flowering has ceased, reduce watering gradually and stop completely when the leaves and stems wither prior to the winter resting period, which lasts from November to February.
Light: Full or half-shade.
Heat: Needs a lot of warmth. Summer, minimum 25°C. (77°F.); autumn, minimum 20°C. (70°F.). The dry tubers should be kept at minimum 15°C. (60°F.) for the winter.

Rechsteineria cardinalis

Air: Very damp air. When spraying, use warm water at minimum 25°C. (77° F.).

Re-potting: Tubers which have been kept dry for the winter ar taken out of the soil in February and replanted in fresh soil. When growth is vigorous, further re-potting may be necessary during the course of the summer.

Propagation: By division of large tubers in February.

Diseases: Watering with water which is too cold produces round, brown spots on the leaves.

Pests: Thrips (when the air is too dry and the light too intense).

NOTE: Always remember to keep the tubers warm and dry in the winter.

Rehmannia angulata

Chinese Foxglove

Habitat: China.

Growth: Perennial with rosettes of large, indented, downy leaves. The flower stems are about 40 cm. (16 in.) high, and bear large purple trumpet-flowers with orange-yellow spots in their throats in May–July.

Use: Ornamental plant for semi-shaded locations in cool rooms.

Soil: Soilless mixture.

Feeding: 2 grams per litre ($\frac{1}{2}$ oz. per gallon) of water every week in spring and early summer.

Water: Keep evenly moist during growth period, after which moderate amounts of water.

Light: Half-shade.

Heat: Cool, airy spot away from draughts; summer, minimum 15°C. (60° F.), winter, minimum 8° C. (47° F.).

Air: Dry indoor air.

Re-potting: Spring, before growth begins. The top withers in the autumn, as with all perennials.

Propagation: By division in spring or by seeding.

NOTE: May be difficult to keep as a permanent indoor plant. Biennial culture may therefore be preferable.

Saintpaulia ionantha   (122)

African Violet

Habitat: Usambara Mountains in Kenya.

Growth: Rosette plant with thick, oval, downy, petiolate leaves. The flowers are gathered into small, loose clusters, 2–6 together, shaped rather like violets. The original type has dark violet flowers with bright yellow anthers. There are varieties, both single and double, with light-blue, white, mauve and pink flowers.

Use: Rewarding, all-year flowering indoor plant, for locations which are not too cool.

Soil: Garden soil, with compost, leaf mould and gravel added. Good drainage. Soilless mixture or other peat-containing mixtures are not particularly suitable.

Feeding: 3 grams per litre (1 oz. per gallon) of water every 2 weeks, in water with the chill taken off it, April–September.

Water: The soil should always be moist, but without retained water. As the plant will not stand moisture being dripped on to leaves and flowers, water into base dishes and pour the excess water away after half an hour. Only use warm water at a minimum 25° C. (80° F.).

Light: Half-shade, but light during the winter. Absolutely no direct sunlight.

Heat: Normal room temperature, but not below minimum 15° C. (60° F.).

Air: Damp air. But avoid spraying, which will produce ugly spots on the leaves. Will not stand draughts.

Re-potting: Spring or early summer, in flat pots.

Propagation: By leaf cuttings in spring.

Diseases: Mildew. Brown ring-marks on the leaves are caused by using water which is too cold.

Sinningia speciosa (123)

Gloxinia

Habitat: Brazil.

Growth: Tuberous plant with short stems which have large, shaggy, velvety, very brittle leaves. The large, bell-shaped flowers are white, red, red with white edges, or blue. Flowering period, May–October.

Use: Lasts longest in a flower window or conservatory with temperature and air humidity maintained at constant levels.

Soil: Equal amounts of peat, leaf mould and sand, possibly a compost mixture.

Feeding: 3 grams per litre (1 oz. per gallon) of water every week from February until flowering begins. No nourishment after that.

Water: Keep the soil evenly moist during the spring and summer, but do not allow to dry out. Use water at a minimum temperature of 25°C. (80°F.). When flowering has ceased in October, reduce the watering gradually, and stop completely when the leaves begin to wither. Dry, warm winter for the tubers until forcing begins in February.

Light: No direct sunshine, best in a semi-shaded location.

Heat: High indoor temperature in growth and flowering periods February–October (minimum 22°C. (75°F.)). Keep the tubers at minimum 15°C. (60°F.) through the winter.

Air: Humid air. Avoid drops of water on leaves and flowers. Avoid draughts.

Re-potting: Put the tubers in flat pots or dishes in February–March and cover them with 2 cm. (1 in.) of soil.

Propagation: By seeding, leaf cuttings or stem cuttings.

Pests: Greenfly.

Diseases: Brown, rolled-up edges caused by air which is too dry.

Varieties: 'Gierts Rote' (red), 'Gierts Weisse' (white), 'Kaiser Friedrich' (scarlet with white edges) and 'Kaiser Wilhelm' (blue with white edges).

Smithiantha hybrida

NOTE: The tubers, which are sold in the same way as those of the Tuberous begonia, may be forced in the identical manner by placing in peat in a warm flower window in February, followed by potting.

Smithiantha hybrida

Habitat: Mexico.

Growth: Tuberous plant, with upright stems, densely covered with down. The heart-shaped, green, downy leaves have dark brown patterns along their veins. The bell-shaped, two-lipped, hanging flowers are borne in petiolate clusters; the upper side is scarlet, the underside yellow and the throat yellow with crimson spots. Flowering period, June–October.

Use: Ornamental, both as a foliage plant and a flower plant. The leaves and stems are brittle, and must be handled with care during transport and daily attention.

Soil: Soilless mixture or leaf mould, with peat and sand mixed in. Good drainage.

Feeding: 3 grams per litre (1 oz. per gallon) of water every 2 weeks, beginning 1 month after the start of growth, and ending when flowering begins.

Water: Large amounts of water at room temperature in spring and summer, until flowering ceases. After that, reduce the amounts gradually until the parts of the plant which are above the surface of the soil wither away. Keep the tubers dry during the winter.

Light: Semi-shaded spot.

Heat: From the time the tuber is planted in March until flowering begins in June, minimum 25°C. (77°F.). During and after flowering, June–October, minimum 20°C. (70°F.). Keep the tuber dry during winter from November to February at minimum 12°C. (55°F.).

Air: Dry air, but will not stand spraying or drops of water on leaves and flowers.

Re-potting: Place the tubers, several together, into a flat dish, and cover with 2 cm. (1 in.) of soil in February.

Propagation: By division of tubers in February.

Pests: Red spider mites and thrips in air which is too dry.

Diseases: Round, brown spots on leaves are caused by watering with water which is too cold.

Streptocarpus hybridus   (124)

Habitat: South Africa.

Growth: Herbaceous biennial with coarse, wrinkled leaves; these are virtually stemless, and collected in a strong rosette. There are 2–3 trumpet-shaped flowers on each stem in white, pink, blue, violet or red, many with veins in other colours and spots on the throat. Often flowers the whole year round.

Use: Good indoor plant, which is easier to cultivate than most other of the *Gesneriaceae.* Attractive flowering in the plant's second year of life.

Soil: Nourishing loam, with the addition of peat and sand, possibly soilless mixture.

Feeding: 3 grams per litre (1 oz. per gallon) of water every week (April–

September). Only give nourishment to damp soil balls.

Water: Plenty in summer, but do not allow to dry out; moderate in winter.

Light: Semi-shaded spot, lighter in winter.

Heat: Normal room temperature, but not less than minimum 15°C. (60°F.).

Air: Preferably damp air in the summer.

Re-potting: February. Take care not to break the very brittle stems.

Propagation: By seed or leaf cuttings.

Pests: Red spider mites (in too much sunshine), greenfly and thrips.

NOTE: One of the best indoor plants for flower windows in semi-shaded locations.

Acanthaceae

Aphelandra squarrosa   (125)

Zebra Plant, Tiger Plant

Habitat: Brazil.

Growth: Tough stem. Large, shiny, pointed, oval leaves, arranged in cross formation, with silvery-white or yellowish markings along the veins. The yellow flowers are collected in a pyramidal inflorescence, each one supported by stiff, yellow bracts. Flowers for 6 weeks between April and August.

Use: Hothouse plant, suitable for conservatories or warm flower windows.

Soil: Heavy, nourishing loam.

Feeding: 3 grams per litre (1 oz. per gallon) of water every week (March–August).

Water: Plenty in summer; winter, moderate.

Light: Semi-shaded location.

Heat: Thrives best at minimum 22°C. (70°F.) the whole year round. At temperatures below 18°C. (65°F.) no flowers will appear. At temperatures above 24°C. (75°F.) the leaves will distort and become unattractive.

Air: High degree of air humidity, otherwise the leaves will roll up.

Re-potting: March.
Cutting: Cut back after flowering has ceased. Otherwise, the plant will tend to become long and spindly.
Propagation: By cuttings in May over a minimum 30° C. (85° F.) bottom heat.
Pests: Scale insects, greenfly.
Diseases: Brown marks on leaves and rolled-up edges are due to air which is too dry, distorted leaves to air temperatures which are too high (over minimum 24° C. (75° F.)).
Varieties: 'Dania' is typical of a few, new, compact varieties with several flower stems. Will stand winter at slightly lower temperatures (minimum 12–15° C. (55–60° F.)), without reduction in the level of flowering.

Beloperone guttata (126)

Shrimp Plant

Habitat: Mexico.
Growth: Evergreen bush with green branches and smooth, pointed, oval leaves. The flowers are white with a purple-red spot on the lower lip, hanging and surrounded by reddish-brown, overlapping bracts in a large, pendulous inflorescence. The individual flowers are not very long-lasting, but the bracts preserve the decorative effect for months on end. Flowers the whole year round. No real resting period.
Use: The only member of the *Acanthaceae* which is suitable for indoor culture. The others are best cultivated in conservatories or greenhouses.
Soil: Porous, strong loam with sand and peat added.
Feeding: 3 grams per litre (1 oz. per gallon) of water every week (February–September). Only give nourishment to damp soil balls.
Water: Moderate the whole year round, without allowing to dry out.
Light: As light as possible, away from direct sunlight. If too strongly shaded, the top leaves will lose their reddish-brown colour.

Crossandra infundibuliformis

Heat: Normal room temperature. Winter, minimum 18° C. (65° F.). If the temperature is too high, the shoots become long and spindly.
Air: Slightly damp air.
Re-potting: February.
Cutting: Occasionally prune top shoots in order to achieve a more compact growth.
Propagation: By top cuttings in April.
Pests: Greenfly.
Diseases: Leaves roll up or fall if the soil ball becomes too dry.
Varieties: 'Nørgards Favorite' with compact growth and dense bracts.

Crossandra infundibuliformis

Habitat: India.
Growth: Low sub-shrub with slightly undulating, shiny, dark green leaves. Upright flower spike with collared, orange flowers. Vigorous and long-flowering, often the whole year round.
Use: Hothouse plant.
Soil: Garden loam, with leaf mould, peat and sand added.
Feeding: 2 grams per litre ($\frac{1}{2}$ oz. per gallon) of water every week (February–September), but never to dry soil balls.
Water: Plenty in summer; winter, moderate, but do not allow to dry out. Use water at minimum 25° C. (77° F.).
Light: Semi-shaded location.

Heat: Summer, minimum 22°C. (72°F.); winter, never below minimum 15°C. (60°F.).

Air: Absolutely damp air. In dry air the leaves will roll up.

Re-potting: February, in flat pots.

Propagation: By cuttings in spring, possibly by seeding.

Pests: Red spider mites.

Diseases: Leaves roll up as a result of dry air or too much light; watering with water which is too cold causes brown spots on leaves.

Varieties: 'Mona Wallhed' with larger, darker and longer-lasting flowers.

NOTE: Unusual flower colour for a pot plant.

Fittonia verschaffeltii   (127)

Habitat: Peru.

Growth: Creeping plant, only 10 cm. (4 in.) high, with oval leaves which have coloured veins. The flower spikes are without ornamental value.

Use: Hothouse plant for ground covering in a warm, damp conservatory or flower window.

Soil: Light, humus-rich soil, leaf mould or sand.

Feeding: 2 grams per litre ($\frac{1}{2}$ oz. per gallon) of water every 2 weeks (March–August).

Water: Keep the soil damp without watering too much.

Light: Shaded or semi-shaded location.

Heat: Minimum 22–25°C. (72–77°F.) the whole year round.

Air: Absolutely damp air. Spray with rain water, which will not produce spots on the leaves.

Re-potting: Spring, in flat pots.

Cutting: Stopping the shoots gives a bushier plant. The flower shoots can be removed when they appear.

Propagation: By cuttings in the spring.

Pests: Slugs and snails, wood lice, greenfly.

Other species: argyroneura (illustrated) with silvery-white leaf veins; *pearcei*

with crimson leaf veins. Planting the two together will give an attractive combination which will provide a 'forest floor' in a warm conservatory.

Jacobinia carnea

Habitat: Brazil.

Growth: Vigorous, square, branched stems. Oval, downy, grey-green leaves. Dense inflorescences with 5 cm. (2 in.) long, rose-red flowers which open simultaneously.

Use: Hothouse plant, flowering in the summer. Best in conservatories.

Soil: Garden loam, rich in humus, or possibly soilless mixture.

Feeding: 2 grams per litre ($\frac{1}{2}$ oz. per gallon) of water every week (March–August).

Water: Plenty the whole year round. The soil balls must never be allowed to dry out.

Light: Semi-shaded location.

Heat: Constant, minimum 20–22°C. (68–74°F.).

Air: Damp air the whole year round.

Re-potting: February, after thorough watering.

Cutting: Stop young plants, so as to obtain more bushy growth. Cut away withered inflorescences.

Jacobinia carnea

Ruellia devosiana

Propagation: By cuttings in spring.
Pests: Greenfly, red spider mites.
Diseases: Rolled up leaf edges are caused by air which is too dry.
Other species: See below.

Jacobinia pohliana

Growth: More vigorous and robust than *Jacobinia carnea*. The leaves are bigger and softer, the inflorescences longer. Use and culture otherwise the same.

Jacobinia paucifolia

Growth: Well-branched stems, growing about 30 cm. (12 in.) high. The nodding tube-like flowers, which are scarlet with yellow tips, are positioned individually on short stems in the axils. Flowers, unlike the other *Jacobinia* types, in late winter (February–April).
Use: Ornamental indoor plant when in flower, winter and early spring.
Culture: As for *Jacobinia carnea*, but does not require quite so much warmth. May sometimes be left out of doors to spend the summer in a warm spot. Bring inside before the first night frost, and place in a cool spot (minimum 10°C. (50° F.)) from October to December. After that, at minimum 18°C. (65° F.) during the flowering period. Re-pot after flowering has ceased in May.

Ruellia devosiana

Habitat: Brazil.
Growth: 30 cm. (12 in.) high, well-branched half-bush. The leaves are oval and pointed with velvety, dark green upper sides having white patterns along the veins, and red undersides. Funnel-shaped, pale mauve flowers, winter and spring.
Use: Best in a shaded flower window with damp air. Worth while both as a foliage plant and a flower plant. Most attractive as an annual.
Soil: Porous soil, rich in humus, with leaf mould, clay and sand added. Good drainage.
Feeding: 1 gram per litre ($\frac{1}{4}$ oz. per gallon) of water every 2 weeks (March–August). The roots become scorched if there is too high a concentration of salt in the soil.
Water: Constantly damp soil. Use water at minimum 25°C. (77° F.).
Light: Semi-shaded location. Will not stand direct sunshine.
Heat: Summer, normal temperature; winter, not below minimum 15°C. (60° F.).
Air: Damp air. Grows badly in central heating. Avoid draughts.
Re-potting: After flowering has ceased in spring, in flat pots.
Cutting: Prune young plants in the summer, to produce compact growth. Older plants are inclined to go bare lower down. They should then be discarded and replaced by young plants from cuttings.
Propagation: By cuttings in June over 25° C. (77° F.) bottom heat.
Pests: Red spider mites, thrips.
Diseases: Rolled-up leaves are the result of too dry air and too much sun.

Thunbergia alata   (128)
Black-eyed Susan

Habitat: South-eastern Africa.
Growth: Perennial, herbaceous, twining plant with decorative, spear-shaped

leaves and large, flat-collared, orange-yellow flowers with blackish-violet throats. Summer-flowering.

Use: May be cultivated as a perennial, but as a rule is treated as an annual, with seeding in the spring. Requires plenty of space in a large-light window with a cord or net trellis. Very rapid growth. Can also be used in a warm spot out of doors.

Soil: Soilless mixture.

Feeding: 3 grams per litre (1 oz. per gallon) of water every week, throughout the growth period.

Water: Plenty; must not dry out completely.

Light: Location as light and airy as possible; full sunlight will do very well.

Heat: Normal summer temperature.

Air: Spraying in hot weather.

Propagation: Seeding in sand and peat in February. The seedlings should be kept evenly moist in a light spot at minimum 15° C. (60° F.).

Re-potting: Transplant to permanent pots when the plants are about 10 cm. (4 in.) high.

Tying up: The trellis must be ready before the plant is taken to its permanent spot. Tie up at the start to avoid the plant tangling.

Cutting: When growth is particularly vigorous, some of the trails must be cut away, in order to assist flowering.

Pests: Red spider mites.

Other species: See below.

Thunbergia grandiflora

Habitat: India.

Growth: Vigorous twining bush with large, slightly bell-shaped, light blue flowers.

Use: Cultivated in large pots or tubs which are planted out in warm conservatories.

Culture: As for *Thunbergia alata*, but not as an annual. Requires more warmth, even during the winter season. Cut back after flowering has ceased in

November. Re-pot after growth begins in early spring.

Labiatae

Coleus blumei   (129)

Coleus

Habitat: Tropical Africa and Asia.

Growth: Square succulent stems. Oval, pointed, saw-toothed leaves with a variety of patterns in many colours. Light-blue flowers in light inflorescences.

Use: Foliage plant, most attractive in its first year.

Soil: Soilless mixture or pure peat with rotten leaves added, pH 4 (very acid soil).

Feeding: 3 grams per litre ($\frac{3}{4}$ oz. per gallon) of water every 2 weeks (March–September).

Water: Moderate the whole year round, less in the resting period, September–January. For preference, use rainwater.

Light: The full colour of the leaves only emerges with strong light, preferably full sunlight, and disappears during the winter.

Heat: Normal room temperature; winter, not below minimum 15° C. (60° F.).

Air: Spray in hot weather.

Re-potting: February, and possibly again in June.

Cutting: Cut back on re-potting in spring, which will counteract the tendency for the lower parts of the stem to become bare.

Propagation: By cuttings or by seeding in February–March.

Pests: Greenfly.

Varieties: Large numbers of varieties with many different leaf colours: 'Bienvenu' (red, with narrow yellow edges), 'Fanal' (dark red), 'Candidum' (whitish-red), 'Pink Rainbow' (salmon pink) and 'Red Rainbow' (red).

NOTE: Best results are obtained in a sunny location; water with rainwater and strong fertiliser.

Other species: See below.

Coleus pumilus

Habitat: Philippines.
Growth: Creeping or hanging stems. The leaves are brown with green edges. There are hybrids and varieties with crimson leaves which have patterns in brown, gold and green. Numerous inflorescences with sky-blue flowers in winter.
Use: Good hanging-bowl plant.
Culture: As for *Coleus blumei*, but require higher temperature and more water in the winter season.

Glechoma hederacea
Ground Ivy

Habitat: Europe (Great Britain).
Growth: Creeping, metre-long (3-ft.) almost wire-like stems. Small, kidney-shaped, round-indented leaves. Upright flower shoots in the axils, and the violet lip-flowers have spots on their throats. Anthers form two crosses. Flowering period, May–June.
Use: Undemanding hanging-bowl plant. May sometimes be left to spend the summer out of doors, e.g. in a balcony-box.
Soil: Leaf mould mixed with sand.

Glechoma hederacea fol. var.

Feeding: 2 grams per litre ($\frac{1}{2}$ oz. per gallon) of water every 2 weeks (April–August).
Water: Summer, normal watering; winter, relatively dry.
Light: Shaded or semi-shaded location.
Heat: Cool room. Winter, minimum 5° C. (40° F.).
Air: Slightly humid air. Spray in hot weather.
Re-potting: Spring, as required.
Propagation: By division.
Variant: foliis variegatis, with white variegated leaves. Greater ornamental value than the main type.

Plectranthus fruticosus

Habitat: South Africa.
Growth: Evergreen sub-shrub, up to a metre (over 3 ft.) high. The leaves are oval, saw-tooth edged and bristly, with reddish stems. When rubbed they give off an aromatic fragrance which was at one time thought to drive away moths. Pale blue flowers in upright clusters in late winter and spring.
Use: Easily satisfied, vigorous plant for indoor locations.
Soil: Garden soil rich in humus.
Feeding: 3 grams per litre (1 oz. per gallon) of water every 2 weeks (April–August).
Water: Moderate the whole year round, least during the resting period, August–January.
Light: Will stand full sunlight.
Heat: Quite indifferent to warmth. In winter, minimum 8° C. (47° F.) is enough, but the plant will stand normal room temperature.
Air: Will stand any indoor air.
Re-potting: Late spring after flowering has ceased.
Cutting: Will take vigorous pruning in the interests of better formation.
Propagation: By cuttings which are taken after flowering.
Pests: Greenfly on young shoots.
Other species: See below.

Plectranthus australis (130)

Habitat: Australia.
Growth: Creeping or hanging stems which are a reddish-brown colour. The leaves are a monotone green on both upper and undersides.
Use: Easily satisfied hanging-bowl plant.
Culture: As for *Plectranthus fruticosus.* Will not stand drying out altogether.

Plectranthus oertendahlii

Growth: Creeping or hanging stems. Dark green leaves with silvery-white stripes along the veins like a net over the surface of the leaf. Pure white flowers in dense, upright clusters in September–October.
Use: Easily satisfied hanging-bowl plant.
Culture: As for *Plectranthus fruticosus.*

Verbenaceae

Clerodendrum thomsoniae

Habitat: Tropical West Africa.
Growth: Summer green, climbing bush, up to 4 m. (13 ft.) high. The leaves are opposite, pointed, oval, and plain-edged. Large flower clusters from March to July. The individual flower consists of a heart-shaped, white calyx, which encloses the blood-red flower, hence the popular name 'Bleeding Heart'. The plant loses its leaves in the resting period, October–February.
Use: Twining indoor plant which needs a strong trellis and a lot of space.
Soil: Light soil, rich in humus.
Feeding: 3 grams per litre (1 oz. per gallon) of water every 2 weeks (March–August).
Water: Summer, normal watering. From September reduce the amounts gradually and leave the plant dry in the winter, as for *Fuchsia.* From February,

more water again and a higher temperature.
Light: Light growth location away from direct sunlight.
Heat: Normal room temperature during growth period. In winter, minimum 5°C. (40°F.). From February, minimum 10°C. (50°F.), rising to normal room temperature.
Air: Frequent spraying, especially in the spring.
Cutting: Prune vigorously on re-potting. The flowers only develop on the year's new shoots. Can be developed as a standard with a trunk by pruning.
Propagation: By cuttings in the spring.
Pests: Red spider mites.
NOTE: Flowering is only satisfactory when the resting period (October–February) is adhered to, and pruning is undertaken subsequently. During the resting time temperature should be minimum 5°C. (40°F.), there should be plenty of light and the plant kept almost dry.
Other species: See below.

Clerodendrum speciosissimum (131)

Growth: Shrub, not a climbing plant. Bright scarlet flowers in large, loose inflorescences in June–September. Black berries.
Use and culture: As for *Clerodendrum thomsoniae,* but does not have quite such a marked resting period. In the first year stopping is omitted, and the plant will then flower at the tip of the main stem.

Clerodendrum fragrans

Growth: Bush form, with white or very pale red flowers which have a soporific fragrance. Flowers the whole year round, with short pauses.
Use and culture: As for *Clerodendrum thomsoniae,* but the winter resting period is unnecessary.

Lantana camara (132)

Habitat: Tropical America.

Growth: Small, deciduous bush, with grey-green, oval leaves. The flowers lie in dense, circular inflorescenses, with the oldest and darkest flowers on the outside, progressively lighter flowers towards the centre and the buds lightest of all. The old flowers wither and fall, and are replaced by the newly opened buds. The duration of the individual inflorescences may range over several months. Often black, berry-like fruits. Varieties are to be found with white, yellow, pink, red and bicoloured (scarlet/orange) flowers.

Use: Long-flowering indoor plant for sunny room. Also, quite suitable for a balcony-box and plant-tub out of doors. Standard plants can be grown.

Soil: Soilless mixture.

Feeding: 3 grams per litre (1 oz. per gallon) of water every week (April–September). Only give nourishment to damp soil balls.

Water: Light, dry soil is to be preferred; hence water sparingly. Never water through a base dish, and make sure there is good drainage from balcony-boxes or plant-tubs.

Light: As much light and sunshine as possible.

Heat: Summer, normal temperature; winter, minimum 10° C. (50° F.).

Air: Dry air, especially during the winter.

Re-potting: February.

Cutting: Older plants may be shaped by stopping the main growths in February. A standard may be formed by allowing a single shoot to run up in the air, supported by a bamboo cane. All side shoots should be removed, and the crown develops where the top shoot is nipped.

Propagation: By cutting in September and/or February.

Pests: Red spider mites.

NOTE: Excellent sunshine plant.

Oleaceae

Jasminum odoratissimum

Habitat: Canary Islands and Madeira.

Growth: Long, slender, green shoots, with 3-segmented leaves. The yellow flowers are produced in small inflorescences, and are delicately fragrant. Flowering is not abundant, but distributed over the whole of the year.

Use: Pot plant or climbing plant, which requires some support.

Soil: Soilless mixture.

Feeding: 2 grams per litre ($\frac{1}{2}$ oz. per gallon) of water every week (March–September).

Water: Even watering the whole year round, but more sparing during the winter.

Light: As much as possible, but not scorching sunshine.

Heat: Normal room temperature.

Air: Spray during the spring.

Re-potting: February.

Cutting: Inclined to shed its bottom leaves. This can be counteracted to some extent by shortening the growths, which will also distribute the flowers more evenly.

Propagation: By cuttings.

Other species: See below.

Jasminum odoratissimum

Jasminum officinale grandiflorum

Habitat: The Orient.
Growth: Small, 5–7-lobed leaves. Pleasant smelling, white flowers in cymes in the shoot tips from June to September.
Use and culture: As for *Jasminum odoratissimum.*

Jasminum polyanthum (133)
Jasmine

Habitat: China.
Growth: Small-lobed leaves on reddish branches. White, powerfully fragrant flowers in the spring. Can be forced into flower up to Christmas.
Use and culture: As for *Jasminum odoratissimum.*

Jasminum mesnyi

Habitat: China.
Growth: Square stems. Three-lobed evergreen leaves. Large yellow flowers in the axils on summer shoots, but no fragrance.
Use and culture: As for *Jasminum odoratissimum.*

Jasminum sambac

Habitat: Eastern Asia, where the flowers are used in temples as offerings to Buddha.
Growth: Upright growth. Oval, pointed leaves. Semi-double, white flowers with a delightful fragrance from early spring until late autumn.
Use and culture: As for *Jasminum odoratissimum,* but requires higher temperature (minimum 25° C. (77° F.)).

Loganiaceae

Nicodemia diversifolia

Habitat: Madagascar.
Growth: Evergreen bush with branching, cinnamon-brown stems and

Nicodemia diversifolia

indented, succulent green leaves, which are reminiscent of oak leaves. No flowering of any significance.
Use: Foliage plant for cool, shady locations, e.g. windows facing north.
Soil: Loam with peat added.
Feeding: 3 grams per litre (1 oz. per gallon) of water every week (April–August).
Water: Summer, plenty; winter, sparingly.
Light: Shade.
Heat: Cool location. Summer, minimum 15° C. (60° F.); winter, minimum 8° C. (47° F.).
Air: Normal indoor air. Spray in hot weather in the summer season.
Re-potting: February.
Cutting: Nip young plants in order to obtain better umbrella-like branching.
Propagation: By cuttings, April–May.
Pests: Red spider mites.

Apocynaceae

Allamanda neriifolia (134)

Habitat: Brazil.
Growth: Tall, slightly twining bush, with evergreen, oleander-like leaves. Large, funnel-shaped, yellow flowers with dark stripes in the funnels. Delicate fragrance.
Use: Best in a light conservatory or large flower window facing south.
Soil: Loam, rich in humus, with the addition of peat, leaf mould and gravel.

Feeding: 5 grams per litre (1½ oz. per gallon) of water every week (April–August).
Water: Plenty of water in summer; winter, moderate.
Light: Light and sunny location.
Heat: Summer, normal room temperature. Winter, not below minimum 15° C. (60° F.).
Air: Damp air with frequent spraying in spring and summer.
Re-potting: February.
Cutting: Cut back old shoots in February.
Propagation: By cuttings over high bottom heat in February.
Pests: Red spider mites.
Other species: See below.

Allamanda cathartica

Growth: Vigorous, twining shrub. Funnel-shaped, yellow flowers with a delicate fragrance.
Use and culture: As for *Allamanda neriifolia.*
Variant: 'Hendersonii', with large bell-shaped, warm-yellow flowers having a delicate fragrance. Reddish buds.

Dipladenia boliviensis

Habitat: Bolivia.
Growth: 2-m. (6-ft.)-high twining plant with smooth, oval leaves. Trumpet-shaped, white flowers with yellow throats, hanging in clusters from the end of the 1-year shoot. Flowering period, May–November.
Use: Long-flowering twining plant for windows facing east or west in not too intense heat.
Soil: Loam, rich in nourishment, with good drainage.
Feeding: 2 grams per litre (½ oz. per gallon) of water every week (April–August). Only give nourishment to damp soil balls.
Water: Summer, normal; winter, moder-

ate. Avoid lingering moisture or water in the base dish.
Light: Light location away from direct sunshine.
Heat: Summer, 16–18° C. (60–65° F.); winter, minimum 14–16° C. (55–60° F.), but not cooler.
Air: Dry indoor air with spraying in summer.
Re-potting: February, in pots which are not too large. Wet thoroughly before re-potting.
Cutting: Cutting back in February will assist the formation of young side shoots which are likely to flower.
Propagation: By cuttings with bottom heat.
Pests: Red spider mites.
Diseases: Curled leaves are the result of too dry air or too intense sunlight.
Other species: See below.

Dipladenia amoena rubiniana

Growth: Vigorous plant with large, scabrous, furrowed, shaggy, almost black-green leaves. The flowers are a deep pink colour.
Use and culture: As for *Dipladenia boliviensis.*

Dipladenia sanderi   (135)

Growth: Shiny, fresh-green leaves. Large, pink flowers with yellow throats.
Use and culture: As for *Dipladenia boliviensis.*
NOTE: This type is often sold in the form of small plants in flower under the name 'Sanderi rosea'. A short time afterwards, they will produce twining runners which must be tied to net or bamboo trellises.

Nerium oleander   (136)
Oleander

Habitat: Mediterranean countries.
Growth: Vigorous, evergreen bush with soft branches and lance-shaped, coriaceous, grey-green leaves. There are also

forms with variegated leaves. The inflorescences grow at the tips of the 1-year shoots. White, pink or red flowers from July until September. Delicate fragrance. *All parts of the plant are highly poisonous.*

Use: Young plants are very suitable for window-sills or flower windows; older plants should be used as tub-plants for conservatories. May sometimes be left out doors for the summer in a warm spot.

Soil: Strong loam with the addition of peat, gravel and a basic fertiliser in the form of bonemeal.

Feeding: 5 grams per litre ($1\frac{1}{2}$ oz. per gallon) of water every week (April–August).

Water: Grows—in the wild state—in river beds which have dried up in the summer, with its roots striking into the damp soil. So, give plenty of water from early spring right through until October. The pot or tub should stand in a spacious base dish, which is filled a few times each week with water at minimum 30° C. (86° F.). It is quite all right to leave water in the dish for long periods. Give more moderate amounts in the winter, but always with the chill taken off.

Light: Likes a lot of light and full sunshine.

Heat: Normal temperature in summer; winter resting period at minimum 5° C. (40° F.).

Air: Dry air. No spraying. When left to spend the summer out of doors the plant should not be exposed to long periods of rain.

Re-potting: February, in spacious pots or tubs. The roots require a lot of space.

Cutting: Prune young shoots. Trunk-trees with 150-cm. (almost 5-ft.) trunks may be trimmed slightly by the removal of all side shoots and suckers.

Propagation: By cuttings in May. May strike roots in water.

Pests: Scale insects, mealy-bugs.

NOTE: The entire plant contains the *deadly poisons*, nerein and oleandrin.

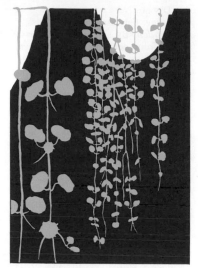

Ceropegia linearis woodii

Asclepiadaceae

Ceropegia linearis woodii

Habitat: Natal.

Growth: Hanging plant with wire-thin runners about a metre (over 3 ft.) long. Heart-shaped, silvery-grey, marbled leaves on short stems. In every axil there are 2–3 flesh-coloured, lantern-shaped flowers. Thickened aerial tubers on the runners. Flowering all year round.

Use: 'Different' hanging plant for windows facing south.

Soil: Very porous soil, e.g. soilless mixture, with sand added.

Feeding: 2 grams per litre ($\frac{1}{2}$ oz. per gallon) of water every 2 weeks (April–July).

Water: Moderate in summer without lingering moisture. Winter, almost completely dry.

Light: Very light location (sun from the south).

Heat: Summer, normal temperature; winter, minimum 8° C. (47° F.). Will not stand high winter temperatures.

Air: Dry air.
Re-potting: February, in small pots.
Propagation: By shoot cuttings, or off-shoots from aerial tubers which will take root.

Hoya bella (137)

Habitat: Java.
Growth: Hanging plant with light, pointed leaves and hanging flower clusters; the long-lasting flowers are pale pink with purple in the centre. Many flowering periods from April to October, with a few weeks' pause in between each.
Use: As a hanging-bowl plant, since the hanging flower clusters must be seen from below for the best effect.
Soil: Good garden soil, with clay, leaf mould and gravel added.
Feeding: 4 grams per litre (1¼ oz. per gallon) of water every 3 weeks (February–July).
Water: Moderate. The roots will not stand too much watering or lingering moisture. From October to January, almost completely dry.
Light: Prefers a semi-shaded location.
Heat: Will stand a high summer temperature. Winter, minimum 15–20° C. (60–70° F.).
Air: Prefers damp air.
Re-potting: Young plants have to be re-potted every spring in February, older plants very seldom. The top layer of soil may need to be renewed (top-dressing).
Propagation: By cuttings in the spring.
Pests: Mealy bugs, scale insects.
Other species: See below.

Hoya carnosa (138)

Wax Flower

Habitat: Eastern Asia.
Growth: Evergreen twining plant with several long (1 m., or more than 3 ft.) greenish-brown shoots with aerial roots. Pointed, oval fleshy, smooth, dark green leaves. Inflorescences develop on small, knotty, perennial stems, which must not be removed since it is here that the next year's flowers are formed. The individual flower is star-shaped, its thick waxy-white petals have a red central spot, and there are 12–15 flowers in every spherical umbel. There is a delicate fragrance, and the blossoms secrete drops of nectar.
Use: Twining plant on firm trellises in windows or against walls, indoors, in conservatories or on verandas.
Culture: As for *Hoya bella,* but prefers dry air and more light. Best in a window facing east or west, possibly a light window facing north, away from direct sunshine. Winter temperature, minimum 12–15° C. (55–60° F.). When the new leaf shoots develop, raise the temperature to 20° C. (70° F.).
Cutting: Old flower stems must not be removed. Long, apparently leafless trails are often formed, which must not be cut away but tied up to the trellis, as they later form leaves in the normal way.
Tying up: Trails are only tied on one side of the trellis, as the plant has a distinct 'front' and 'back', and always turns the upper surface of the leaves to the one side.

Stapelia variegata

Habitat: South Africa.
Growth: Succulent, with finger-thick, upright shoots. The flower is shaped like a 5-cornered star, and is light brown with dark brown spots in attractive patterns. When it emerges it has a distinct carrion smell, which attracts flies to lay eggs in it, therefore the fly larvae take care of the flower's pollination.
Use: Very suitable for cactus windows in full sunshine from the south.
Soil: Cactus soil with clay, sand, peat and crocks. Good drainage.
Feeding: 2 grams per litre (½ oz. per gallon) of water every 3 weeks (March–July).

Stapelia variegata

Water: Spring and summer, moderate watering with drying-out in between. From September gradually reduce the quantities. In winter, almost completely dry.
Light: Sunshine.
Heat: Summer, normal room temperature; winter, minimum 8°C. (47° F.).
Air: Dry indoor air.
Re-potting: Seldom.
Propagation: By shoot cuttings in the spring.

Stephanotis floribunda (139)

Habitat: Madagascar.
Growth: Vigorous twining plant with several shoots about a metre (over 3 ft.) long. The dark green leaves are oval and coriaceous, and in the axils are 8–10 white, fragrant, tubular flowers with flat lobes. Flowering period, May–October.
Use: Twining plant for trellises and walls indoors, in conservatories and on verandas.
Soil: Soilless mixture.
Feeding: 3 grams per litre (1 oz. per gallon) of water every week (March–October).
Water: Needs a lot of water during the growth and flowering periods. Must never be allowed to dry out, but should never have standing water in the base dish. Winter, moderate watering, without extended periods of drought.
Light: Windows facing east or west.
Heat: Summer, normal temperature; winter, minimum 12–15°C. (55–60° F.).
Air: Dry air.
Re-potting: January, in pots which are not too small.
Tying up: Tie up young shoots regularly, so that the leaves and flowers can unfold freely. The plant has a tendency to flower in the tips of new shoots (right up at the top), therefore the trellising should be arranged so that the young shoots are distributed evenly over the whole of the plant.
Propagation: By cuttings over 25°C. (77° F.) minimum bottom heat, in the spring.
Pests: Scale insects, mealy bugs.
Diseases: Yellow spots on leaves are the result of too harsh sunlight; leaves turning completely lemon-yellow are the result of drought.

Rubiaceae

Bouvardia domestica

Habitat: Central America.
Growth: Evergreen bush with opposite leaves. The flowers are tubular, with 4-lobed collars, and are velvety on the outer sides. There are varieties in shades of white, pink and red. Flowering period, June–December.
Use: Flowering indoor plant for a light window or conservatory.
Soil: Strong loam with added peat, leaf mould and sand. pH 6·5.
Feeding: 2 grams per litre ($\frac{1}{2}$ oz. per gallon) of water every week (April–September).
Water: Summer, plenty; after flowering, sparingly.
Light: Window facing east or west.
Heat: Summer, warm (minimum 25°C. (77° F.)); autumn and winter, minimum 16°C. (60° F.). Flowers are long-lasting in relatively low temperature.
Air: Frequent spraying during the growth period.
Re-potting: Spring.

Cutting: Stopping main shoots in May will give better branching and a large number of flowers.
Propagation: By cuttings in April–May.
Pests: Greenfly, scale insects.
Diseases: Grey mould.
Other species: See below.

Bouvardia longifolia humboldtii (140)

Growth: A taller plant than the last species, with shining, rather leathery dark green leaves, and much larger fragrant white flowers which are up to 4 cm. (1½ in.) long and 2·5 cm. (1 in.) across, borne in less dense corymbs. Flowering period, September–December.
Use and culture: As for *Bouvardia domestica*, but will thrive under cooler conditions; summer, minimum 16°C. (60°F.); winter, minimum 13°C. (55°F.).

Coffea arabica (141)

Coffee

Habitat: Tropical Africa.
Growth: Branchy bush, with opposite, shiny, dark green leaves. Plants 3–4 years old have a profusion of star-shaped, fragrant white flowers from July to September. Cherry-like fruit, first green, then red and finally black, each one with two 'coffee beans'.
Use: Suitable for a large flower window in a semi-shaded location, in a conservatory or hall.
Soil: Soilless mixture with good drainage.
Feeding: 3 grams per litre (1 oz. per gallon) of water every 2 weeks (March–October).
Water: Plenty in summer, winter moderate. Will not stand lingering moisture.
Light: Semi-shaded location.
Heat: Normal room temperature with no major fluctuations, the whole year round. Soil temperature must never drop below 15°C. (60°F.).

Air: Damp air.
Re-potting: February–March, in spacious pots.
Cutting: Young plants have a single upright trunk with horizontal side branches, older plants are more branched. The plant can be adapted to the dimensions of the growth situation by nipping.
Propagation: By seeding completely fresh seeds over a minimum 25°C. (77°F.) bottom heat in March, or by cuttings of top shoots (*not* side shoots).
Pests: Mealy bugs, scale insects. Wash the leaves down regularly.

Gardenia jasminoides (142)

Gardenia

Habitat: Eastern Asia.
Growth: Evergreen bush with pointed, oval, full-edged, shiny leaves and white to yellowish-white double flowers with a delicate fragrance. Flowering period, May–October.
Use: Best in light window facing east or west.
Soil: Humus-rich loam, with peat and sand added. pH 3·5 (very acid soil).
Feeding: 4 grams per litre (1¼ oz. per gallon) of water every 2 weeks (March–August). Only give nourishment to damp soil balls.
Water: Evenly damp soil the whole year round. Only use rainwater at minimum 20°C. (70°F.). If mains water containing calcium is to be used, add 1 gram of ammonium sulphate per litre (¼ oz. per gallon). The soil should never dry out, but must also never remain damp and cold. Water must never be left in the base dish.
Light: Light window facing east or west.
Heat: The ideal mean temperature the whole year round is minimum 16°C. (60°F.), as bud formation takes place at this temperature. Below a minimum 16°C. (60°F.), the buds do not form properly; above 18°C. (65°F.), the bud development is retarded in favour of leaf growth and the buds are shed. In the

vegetative period the temperature may be allowed to rise to 25° C. (77° F.).

Air: Maintain constantly damp air, especially in spring and early summer. Frequent spraying at these times of the year, but not during the winter.

Re-potting: February. Firm planting at the same depth as previously.

Propagation: By cuttings over minimum 25° C. (77° F.) bottom heat in March or September.

Pests: Scale insects, mealy bugs.

Diseases: Yellow leaves are the result of watering with water which contains too much calcium and/or is too cold.

Variants: *fortunei,* with vigorous growth, large leaves and large, double flowers; *plena,* the most commonly seen, double flowered; and *veitchii,* which also has double flowers in the winter.

Ixora coccinea (143)

Ixora·

Habitat: East Indies.

Growth: Evergreen bush with shiny, elliptical leaves, and large, semi-spherical flower umbels having orange-red or salmon-red flowers in the summer.

Use: Attractive, summer-flowering plant for light flower windows and conservatories. Will not stand being moved during flowering. Newly purchased plants often shed their flowers when they are placed indoors. Repeated flowering after acclimatisation.

Soil: Acid humus soil with peat and sand added. pH 4.

Feeding: 3 grams per litre (1 oz. per gallon) of water every week (March–August). Requires a great deal of nourishment in order to flower.

Water: Summer, normal watering without drying out and without lingering water; winter, moderate. Use only rainwater warmed to room temperature; if lime-containing mains water is used, add 1 gram of ammonium sulphate per litre ($\frac{1}{4}$ oz. per gallon).

Light: A lot of light, but away from direct sunlight from the south.

Heat: High room temperature; winter, not below minimum 18° C. (65° F.). Soil temperature should also not be allowed to fall below 18° C. (65° F.).

Air: Damp air with frequent spraying.

Re-potting: February. Older plants should not be re-potted every year.

Cutting: Stop leading shoots frequently during the growth period, as this will assist the spreading of branches. When the flower buds appear, cease nipping.

Propagation: By soft cuttings over minimum 25° C. (77° F.) bottom heat in April.

Pests: Mealy bugs, scale insects.

Diseases: Rolled-up leaves are a sign of too much sunlight; yellowing or falling leaves are indicative of too low a soil temperature or of watering with water which is too cold.

Manettia inflata (144)

Habitat: Tropical America.

Growth: Twining sub-shrub with oval, fresh-green leaves. The tube-like scarlet flowers have short, yellow crown lobes. Flowers throughout the summer and often throughout the year.

Use: Twining plant for light, not too warm flower windows or conservatories.

Soil: Earth mould, rich in nourishment, with peat and sand added.

Feeding: 2 grams per litre ($\frac{1}{2}$ oz. per gallon) of water every week (February–October).

Water: Summer, plenty; winter, moderate, but without drying out. Use rainwater or softened mains water.

Light: Plenty, but away from direct sunlight.

Heat: High indoor temperature. It is important that the soil temperature should not drop below minimum 18° C. (65° F.).

Air: Damp air with frequent spraying, spring and summer.

Re-potting: February. Older trellis

Lonicera japonica aureoreticulata

plants are difficult to re-pot. Instead, top dressing can be given, but taking care not to damage the roots.
Cutting: Cutting back after flowering has ceased will assist the new growth.
Tying up: Young plants must be tied up to a wire gauze or bamboo trellis.
Propagation: By cuttings over minimum 25° C. (77° F.) bottom heat.
Pests: Greenfly.
Diseases: Yellow leaves are due to cold and damp soil or to using water which is too cold.

Caprifoliaceae

Lonicera japonica aureoreticulata

Habitat: Japan.
Growth: Almost evergreen, twining plant with reddish stems and small, oval, pointed leaves, which are green with a network of yellow veins.
Use: Decorative trellis or hanging-bowl plant for rooms, conservatories and—under favourable conditions—out of doors (trellis facing south, with some sort of winter covering).
Soil: Loam with peat and sand added. pH 6.

Feeding: 2 grams per litre ($\frac{1}{2}$ oz. per gallon) of water every week during the growth period.
Water: Summer, plenty; and no drying out. Winter, almost dry.
Light: Window facing east, west or north. In deep shade the vein patterns on the leaves are reduced.
Heat: Cool room temperature. Winter, minimum 8° C. (45° F.).
Air: Fresh, airy spot.
Re-potting: Spring, before growth begins.
Cutting: Cut back, especially the thin shoots, in February.
Tying up: Should be tied to bamboo canes or trellis wire, before the trails become tangled with one another. Can also be cultivated as a hanging plant.
Propagation: By cuttings in spring and summer.
Pests: Red spider mites, greenfly.

Viburnum tinus (145)

Laurustinus

Habitat: Mediterranean countries.
Growth: Evergreen bush with compact growth. Elliptical, shiny, dark green leaves. White or pale pink, fragrant flowers gathered into a rounded umbel. Normal flowering in May, but can be forced from February to March.
Use: Tub plant in conservatories. Can be left to spend the summer in a warm spot out of doors.
Soil: Strong, loam soil, rich in nourishment, with sand and gravel added. Good drainage.
Feeding: 3 grams per litre (1 oz. per gallon) of water every week (March–September).
Water: Summer, plenty. Winter, just enough water to prevent the soil from drying out. Leaves are shed, if completely dry.
Light: Light and airy spot; will stand full sunlight very well.
Heat: Summer, normal temperature. From November to January, minimum

5° C. (40° F.), after that slow forcing at minimum 12° C. (55° F.).
Air: Dry air. Only spray during spring forcing.
Re-potting: At intervals of 1 year, after flowering has ceased in May. At the same time the roots can be pruned to avoid having to use too big tubs.
Cutting: The plant is shaped by stopping young shoots.
Propagation: By cuttings in April or August.
Pests: Greenfly, mealy bugs, scale insects.

Campanulaceae

Campanula isophylla   (146–147)

Habitat: Italy.
Growth: Perennial with thin, hanging, very fragile stems, which exude a milky sap when lacerated. The short-stemmed grey-green leaves are down-covered. Large, open, star-shaped flowers.
Use: Well-known, easily satisfied indoor plant for window-sills or hanging-bowls. Can also be used as ground cover in conservatories, or—in the summer—out of doors in a balcony-box or flower-tub. Cultivated as an annual.
Soil: Strong, alkaline garden soil with gravel added.
Feeding: 2 grams per litre ($\frac{1}{2}$ oz. per gallon) of water every week (April–July).
Water: Summer, plenty of water. From September, very dry. If kept for the winter, the plant should be kept light, dry and cool (minimum 5° C. (40° F.)).
Light: Very well-lit location. Full sunlight will do very well.
Heat: Cool room temperature. Winter, minimum 5° C. (40° F.). If kept warm during the winter, only a few flowers will be obtained.
Air: Normal indoor air.
Re-potting: February.
Propagation: By cuttings or division in the spring.

Diseases: Grey-mould and other fungus diseases are the result of soil or air which are too damp. Withering disease: Cause unknown, affected plants should be thrown out.
Variants: alba, with white flowers, and 'Mayii', with blue flowers and variegated leaves.

Compositae

Chrysanthemum morifolium hortorum   (148)

Chrysanthemum

Habitat: China.
Growth: Perennial with woody base and vigorous stems. The more or less indented leaves are dark green with pale undersides. The single daisy-shaped—or more or less double—flowers are to be found in all colours, except blue and violet.
Use: Vigorous varieties are used in gardens, cool houses or cool conservatories, planted out in the open or in pots; low, short-day treated types in pots as decoration indoors or on a balcony.
Soil: Heavy earth mould with gravel added. Good drainage.
Feeding: Plants in gardens and conservatories: 5 grams per litre ($1\frac{1}{2}$ oz. per gallon) every week from spring until flowering begins. Flowering indoor plants: no nourishment.
Water: Large consumption of water, especially in sunshine and warmth.
Light: Light and sunny spot.
Heat: Cool, especially during flowering. Should spend the winter at minimum 2° C. (36° F.). Short-day treated plants should be thrown out after flowering has ceased.
Air: Absolutely dry air.
Re-potting: Spring.
Cutting: Stopping the main shoot early in the year will produce bushy plants with a number of small flowers. If side shoots are rubbed off and the main heads restricted to one bud, there will be

Gerbera jamesonii

few flowers, but they will be large ones. This method is only to be used for the large-flowering varieties.
Propagation: By cuttings in the spring, or by division of older plants.
Pests: Greenfly.
Diseases: Mildew in too damp air.
NOTE: Short-day treated plants can be induced to flower at any time of the year by means of artificial 'short days' produced by keeping them in the dark or by giving extra light, as the case may be, in forcing houses. Such plants cannot be forced a second time, and should be thrown out after flowering has ceased indoors or in a conservatory.

Gazania splendens   (149)

Habitat: South Africa.
Growth: Low perennial with long, narrow leaves having white felt undersides and rolled-up edges. The flowers are large and marguerite-shaped, with yellow- or orange-edged crowns having a dark, eye-like pattern at the base; they only open in sunlight. Flowers the whole summer long.
Use: Flower plant for sunny windows facing south, conservatories or balcony-boxes or plant-tubs out of doors. Cultivated as a rule as an annual.

Soil: Soilless mixture.
Feeding: 2 grams per litre ($\frac{1}{2}$ oz. per gallon) of water every week (April–September).
Water: Normal.
Light: Full sunlight.
Heat: High summer temperature. May possibly be allowed to winter at minimum 5° C. (40° F.).
Air: Dry air.
Re-potting: March–April.
Propagation: By cuttings in August, like *Pelargonia*.

Gerbera jamesonii

Habitat: South Africa.
Growth: Perennial with deep roots. Dandelion-like leaves, in rosettes and covered with down. The flowers grow on leafless stems; the ray florets are long and pointed in white, yellow, red and all intermediate shades. The disk-flowers are yellow.
Use: Tub-plant for a conservatory. Can be left to spend the summer in a warm spot out of doors.
Soil: Sandy loam with peat added. pH 7·5. Use deep pots and tubs, since the roots penetrate to a depth of 50 cm. (20 in.). Good drainage.
Feeding: 2 grams per litre ($\frac{1}{2}$ oz. per gallon) every week, April–August.
Water: Summer, plenty, without drying out; winter, moderate.
Light: Sunny spot.

Ligularia tussilaginea

Heat: Summer, normal temperature. During the resting period in October–February, minimum 10°C. (50°F.), after which force at minimum 15°C. (60°F.).
Air: Normal dry air. During the growth period, however, spray frequently, but without wetting the flowers.
Re-potting: February, in deep pots or tubs.
Propagation: By seeding or division.
Pests: Greenfly, red spider mites.
Diseases: Fungus, which produces rot, is caused by cold, damp soil.

Ligularia tussilaginea

Habitat: Japan.
Growth: Herbaceous plant with long-stemmed, coltsfoot leaves, which are a glistening green colour with yellow spots and patterns. Yellow flowers have no ornamental value.
Use: Easily satisfied indoor or conservatory plant which will stand shade.
Soil: Soilless mixture in large, deep pots.
Feeding: 3 grams per litre (1 oz. per gallon) of water every week during the growth period.
Water: Summer, plenty; from October to February, very dry.
Light: Thrives in windows facing north.
Heat: Summer, normal room temperature; winter, minimum 15°C. (60°F.).
Air: Will stand dry indoor air.
Re-potting: February.
Propagation: By division in February.

Senecio cruentus   (150)
Cineraria

Habitat: Canary Islands.
Growth: Herbaceous plant with large, heart-shaped, downy, dark green leaves. The composite flowers are collected into large inflorescences, which almost cover the foliage. All colours are represented. Flowering period from February to June, but the individual plants flower only for about 6 weeks indoors.

Senecio mikanioides

Use: Biennial indoor plant, which is thrown out after flowering has ceased.
Soil: Soilless mixture, best in plastic pots with low evaporation.
Feeding: No need to give nourishment during the short period the plant will be indoors.
Water: Large amounts, on hot days often twice a day; may be watered in a base dish. Must never be allowed to dry out.
Light: Light window. Best facing east or west. Strong sunlight will cause the colours to fade and will shorten the flowering period.
Heat: Cool (minimum 10–15°C. (50–60°F.).
Air: Spray in hot weather.
Re-potting: Throw the plant out after it has ceased flowering.
Propagation: By seed.
Pests: Greenfly, especially in draughts and sunlight. Spray the plant thoroughly or throw out when seriously affected by pest attack. The plant is often colloquially called 'bug plant'. Leaf miner.
Other species: See below.

Senecio mikanioides
German Ivy

Habitat: South Africa.
Growth: Climbing or hanging plant, with thin, ivy-like, light green leaves. Very rapid growth. Flowers have no ornamental value.
Use: Hanging plant for cool rooms, e.g. conservatories, verandas or staircases.
Soil: Soilless mixture.
Feeding: 2 grams per litre ($\frac{1}{2}$ oz. per

gallon) of water every week (March–October).

Water: Summer, plenty; winter, moderate.

Light: Window facing north, or other shaded place.

Heat: Cool indoor air; winter, at the most 15° C. (60° F.).

Air: Dry air.

Re-potting: February.

Cutting: Cut back in February.

Propagation: By cuttings. The plant rapidly goes bare at its base, which is why frequent replacement by new plants is recommended.

Pests: Greenfly.

INDEX

Colour illustrations are indicated by *italic* figures.